D1280041

MASTERS
in
MINIATURE
VOLUME I

12
ARTISANS AT WORK

Anne Day Smith

MASTERS *in* MINIATURE

VOLUME I

12
ARTISANS AT WORK

Anne Day Smith

Kalmbach Miniatures, Inc.
Milwaukee, Wisconsin

To Gerry, my in-house editor,
for his love and encouragement
to always do my best.

Copyright 1987 by Anne Day Smith

ISBN 0-933168-81-0

All rights reserved. No portion of this book may be reproduced in any form without the written permission of Kalmbach Miniatures, Inc.

Printed in the United States of America, by Benton Review Printing. Edited by Sybil Harp. Cover and inside page design by Jack Gordon. Art production by Jan Crerie.

Except where otherwise indicated, all photographs are by Chris Becker.

Author's Acknowledgements

I felt a little bit like an explorer, albeit a modern-day one, as I set out across the country to visit the artisans chosen for this book. From the Atlantic coast to the Pacific, from the Northeast to the Southwest, and between, I was privileged to visit the homes and workshops of these diverse and talented artisans. In each case, I was received with genuine warmth and courtesy.

If there is a common thread linking these artisans, I think it is that they are dedicated to their work, committed to striving for quality in the mediums they have chosen, and proud of their accomplishments to date, while eager to explore and expand their capabilities.

I wish to thank each one for his, and her, complete cooperation in this project.

I also wish to especially thank Chris Becker for his exceptional photographs. His professional eye and unique skill with his camera have added a significant dimension to this project. Our thanks, too, to the collectors who allowed him to photograph their treasured objects.

And special thanks to Sybil Harp, the Editor who has taken this project from a mere, wouldn't-it-be-nice, idea to its successful completion with her usual, positive and unflappable professionalism.

Anne Day Smith

Editor's Acknowledgements

I wish to thank the collectors and artisans who shared their unique perspectives with me while this project was in the planning stage, and who were so encouraging throughout its completion.

I especially wish to thank the members of the ad hoc committee who helped with the selection of artisans for this volume of *Masters in Miniature,* which I hope will be the first of many.

I also want to thank Mel Frantz, Editor of *Nutshell News,* for lightening the load for me when I had conflicting deadlines.

A note of thanks is due Norm Nielson of Norm's Dollhouse in Littleton, Colorado, for making the room settings used in photographing Ralph Partelow's pianos.

And I give heartfelt thanks to my many friends in the miniatures field — artisans, manufacturers, collectors, writers, and others — for their patience, encouragement and support throughout the past year. I can personally attest to the truth of the oft-repeated statement that ''miniatures people'' are among the nicest to be found on the face of the earth.

Sybil Harp

Painting, "The Courtesan Nakagawa" by Marjorie Adams;
rug and needle point in progress by Sharon Garmize; wine flask
and glasses by Francis Whittemore; silver wine cooler
by Peter Acquisto.

Introduction

Since the beginning, they have been an essential part of our everyday existence, weaving the fabric of human life, transforming raw material into civilized form. They are the artisans.

They are the cabinetmakers and carpenters, the carvers and joiners. They are the silversmiths and goldsmiths, the blacksmiths and tinsmiths. They are the glassmakers and shoemakers, the potters and pewterers. They are the spinners and weavers, the creators and beautifiers.

Gracefully, gently, often elegantly, these artisans coax form and function from their respective mediums. Utilitarian objects become art in their hands.

It is the artisans and craftsmen who give substance to each new civilization. Their work shapes our thoughts and desires. Over generations they have copied and adapted, refined and enhanced our surroundings, and expanded our horizons. In sometimes subtle ways these artisans have taken the best of what has gone before and added a new interpretation or dimension. It is a uniquely individual process.

An artisan creates and a part of himself goes into his work. When the finished work leaves his hands, a part of himself goes with it, to remain with it always. The finished work will forever be his own.

To say that someone excels at what he or she does is to say that you admire his work, you admire the way he approaches and transforms his medium. Through admiration comes understanding of the artisan's interpretation of his medium. The intrinsic value of the piece becomes more and more evident. This is especially true in the world of miniatures, where handcrafting has been brought to higher and higher levels of excellence. Through design and crafting, the work of miniatures artisans encompasses all the techniques and disciplines that have gone before.

The handcrafting of miniatures has been in existence since earliest recorded history. Thousands of years ago miniature versions of full-size people were crafted to be buried with the Egyptian Pharaohs, to continue serving in their occupations just as their living models had done while the Pharaoh was alive. Along with them were all the accouterments of the Pharoah's life on earth, also in miniature size. Examples of chariots, furniture, kitchen utensils, all have been found in the tombs. It is believed that these items were as accurate in their miniature size as it was possible to produce because they were intended to be used, not merely to be looked at. Thus began a tradition of realism in the creation of miniatures that has endured throughout their history.

Although the size of a work of art cannot be the only criteria by which that work is judged, it is the miniature form that has always held a special fascination that cannot be denied. Miniature versions of a larger work exemplify the artisan's ability to apply both control and freedom to the work. To simply reduce the measurements of a piece does not necessarily result in a perfect miniature. All of the parts of the work must be in proportion to each other. It is the master of his medium who can produce this optical illusion.

The artisans today who achieve this high level of excellence truly are considered "masters in miniature." Some of them, by no means all of them, are featured in this book.

If there is a common denominator among these contemporary master artisans, it is that they are each in harmony with their respective mediums. Their high standards and professional integrity are well known and appreciated.

We salute their various abilities to create, to transform raw material into art, just as generations have before us. May it always be so.

Top: Half-inch scale piano by Ralph Partelow; cat by Charles and Ferbie Claudon. Above left: Porcelain bust by Marty Saunders; painting, "The Artist's Sister," by Marjorie Adams. Above right: Figure by Marty Saunders; cat by Charles Claudon.

The Artisans

Peter Acquisto

Let each man pass his days in that wherein his skill is greatest.
—Sextus Aurelius Propertius (54 B.C.-A.D.2)

Paul Revere's name is synonymous with silver, but when you say "silver" to miniaturists, many of them immediately think of Peter Acquisto. It has been his special medium for the past seventeen years.

Pete was born in Espanola, New Mexico, the son of a Sicilian father and a mother whose Hispanic ancestors lived in the area long before historical records were kept. Pete's early childhood was spent in California, but the family moved back to Albuquerque when Pete was ten, and he has lived there ever since.

A somewhat reticent artist when it comes to talking about himself, Pete would rather discuss and show visitors around his lovely city. He is a knowledgeable guide, and it is obvious that he derives both personal pleasure and professional satisfaction from living where he does.

Albuquerque, a high desert city with an elevation about the same as Denver's, is surrounded by mountains which provide spectacular views

Fine craftsmanship is in the blood of Peter Acquisto, whose Sicilian father was a furniture maker. For a time Pete worked with him in business, and together father and son made several pieces of furniture, including the chair pictured at right, which was built by Pete and carved by his father. Later Pete branched off on his own and turned his talents toward silver, first in jewelry making and later in creating the fine miniatures tableware and accessories for which he is noted. Pictured above, top, is a chamber candlestick shown with a footed shell dish, salver and two sterling mugs. The three-footed salver in the photo immediately above is copied from a Paul Revere ii design and the goblets are reproduced from originals made in England. The prototype for each piece of Acquisto silver is made of brass. "It's an easy metal to work with," Pete believes.

in every direction. On one side, rising abruptly to 10,000 feet, are the Sandia Mountains where Pete and his wife, Dee, enjoy hiking. They often take the aerial tramway to the top, and walk down the five-mile trail.

Descending that trail, they can see all of their city spread out before them. From its Spanish colonial beginnings in 1706, Albuquerque has grown to fill almost the whole valley, and now has a population of some half-million people. It is a city that combines its Hispanic culture with its Indian origins, resulting in unique forms of artistic expression and giving the city an almost foreign flavor.

A tour of the city usually starts in Old Town, where the city began along the Rio Grande river. The life of the community centered around the Plaza and the San Felipe de Neri church which is still serving its people today, after almost two hundred years. Other restored buildings around the Plaza are shops and food establishments, and each has a covered walkway facing the plaza. It is along many of these that the Indians spread out their wares for sale, on colorful blankets.

There is a selection of pottery and woven Navajo rugs or blankets, but the most popular displays for many

visitors are of silver. As we walk, Pete explains the intricacies and origins of the designs typical of the Navajo tribes, or the Zunis, or other Pueblo people who display their wares here. These selections are mostly smaller jewelry items such as rings, bracelets and necklaces. Many are adorned with turquoise, of course, which is indigenous to this region, but jade and coral are also used. Pete can tell you how each of these stones is cut and polished, and finally incorporated into a work of art. He has a hands-on familiarity with each step in the process.

Seventeen years ago, when Pete

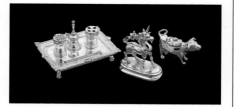

Frances De Rael Acquisto (left), known as Dee to her friends, models some of the silver and turquoise jewelry her husband made especially for her. Pictured above, top, are an ink well set, a unicorn, and a cow pitcher. One of the tools Pete uses in making such intricately detailed pieces is called an escapement file. "They're so fine you can hardly feel them," he explains. "These are the best files you can buy." The candelabrum shown above, a copy of one in the Metropolitan Museum of Art, is made in two parts, in one-inch and half-inch scales.

was twenty and newly-married, he was working with his father in the family woodworking business. They built and handcarved furniture, restored antique pieces, and even did upholstering. "But I didn't like it because I was allergic to the sawdust," Pete admits today. He and a friend decided to open a jewelry business.

In the beginning, Pueblo Indian Jewelry was buying the handmade jewelry and re-selling it. Then Pete and his partner decided "we might as well try to make some of the simple pieces," he remembers, so they hired an Indian silversmith with the daunting name of Whirling Wind. "It wasn't his real name," Pete laughs, "but he thought it sounded good." Pete's partner took over the selling,

and Pete sat down with Whirling Wind to learn the craft of handmade jewelry.

> *"We could have been millionaires now if we hadn't been young and foolish"*

Starting with "very simple things at first," Pete recalls, he gradually progressed to the point where he could make "rings, bracelets, pendants, anything we needed." As the Indian craftsman worked on the more intricate details, it was Pete's task to prepare the basic shape of the piece,

the shank of a bracelet perhaps. "It saved him time," Pete notes, "and it was something anyone could do." Using turquoise and other stones they had learned to cut and polish themselves, Pete was soon soldering the parts of each piece of jewelry into place, only one of the techniques he still uses today.

"It took me a little longer because I like everything done perfectly," Pete admits, "so I was kind of slow. That was my only problem." The demand for the jewelry was growing faster than Pete and Whirling Wind could produce it, so additional silversmiths were hired, and Pete added workshop space to the small house where the business had started. "I was training the silversmiths myself," Pete explains, "because we had developed our own style of making the jewelry."

At its peak, the business employed almost 60 people. A subsidiary,

Enthusiasts of the arts and crafts of their native Southwest, Pete and Dee collect kachina dolls (right). The White Buffalo dancer on the right in the photo is probably the most important one in their collection. The tea set pictured above, top, which includes a tea pot, sugar bowl, cream pot, waste bowl and tray, is representative of the ornate pieces that Pete prefers to make, partly because they offer so much challenge. Among his simpler work is the place setting above, which includes the ca. 1755 plate that was one of Pete's first miniature pieces.

Southwest Casting, was started, and Pete bought a casting machine to help produce some parts of the jewelry. It was a busy and exciting time for these young men. In fact, "we could have been millionaires now if we hadn't been young and foolish," Pete believes.

Still in their early twenties, they bought "new cars every year. At one time I had five different vehicles," Pete recalls. They took their families on vacations to Hawaii and California, casually picked up the tab for restaurant dinners for ten or fifteen friends at a time. It was in California that they endured one of the business' most serious setbacks. While they were dining in a restaurant to celebrate that day's successful sales, their hotel room was broken into and all of the rest of their jewelry, several cases full and worth about $60,000 at wholesale, was stolen.

Over the next few years there were other incidents and adventures related to the business, and Pete had several different partners during that time. His last partner was on the road, selling to customers in Las Vegas, when he was robbed, and stabbed in the process. He managed to assist in the arrest of the thief and get himself to the hospital where, "he called and told me he quit," Pete remembers.

Pete bought his partner's interest in the business just before Indian jewelry suddenly declined in popularity. "I was in a pretty bad position," Pete recalls, "because I had all this jewelry and nobody wanted it." Then he learned that there was still a market for it in Alaska, "so I made three trips to Alaska and sold everything I had up there," he says.

The trend in jewelry design then was becoming more contemporary,

and at first Pete followed that trend, but he didn't enjoy making and selling that type of jewelry nearly as much as he had the more traditional, Indian jewelry. "I just couldn't get enthusiastic about it," Pete admits. "If you believe in something, you can sell it. If you don't..."

Pete was making jewelry components for other craftsmen, supplying only parts of the pieces and not having to worry about selling something he didn't believe in, when his sister Jeanette Vines suggested he use his skills to create miniature silver. Although he admired the work she was doing, Pete admits that he "wasn't too interested" in her suggestion when they first talked about it in 1978, "and didn't really pursue it" at the time."

About a year later, Jeanette was planning to send some of the upholstered furniture she makes with a

friend who was going to a show in Chicago. She asked Pete again, ''Why don't you make some pieces and my friend will take them and show them around?'' Pete remembers, ''So I said, okay. We made three pieces, pretty simple things, a coffee pot, a plate and a goblet.''

A Chicago shop-owner saw these first pieces, and decided to order a dozen of each, telling Pete she was going to send them to select customers on approval. ''Everybody accepted the pieces and they ordered more of the goblets and the plates,'' Pete recalls now. ''So she called me right away with another order.'' It was this initial indication of interest that caused Pete to decide that ''maybe we'd better get a little more involved in this,'' he smiles as he remembers the incident.

When Pete says ''we,'' he is referring to his wife, Dee, who often travels with him to shows, and who is involved in the part of the business Pete enjoys the least, the final finishing or washing and polishing of each piece of Acquisto silver.

Dee was born and brought up in Japan, the daughter of a Japanese mother and an American father whose Hispanic heritage can be traced back to the earliest settlers of New Mexico. Dee and her parents came home to Albuquerque when she was 16. She has lived there ever since, and has retained her ability to understand and speak Japanese. Dee was a student at the University of New Mexico when she and Pete married in 1970.

Now Dee is one of the six people who are involved in the intricate process of creating Acquisto miniature

Pete and Dee enjoy hiking in the mountains (above) that surround their home city of Albuquerque. Pete selects many of the pieces he creates (left) from his large collection of books about silver.

silver. Pete trains each of them, usually for up to six months, before they are able to work at the standard he requires. He admits that ''I want them to do great work from the beginning, which is impossible.'' Pete allows time in his own schedule to ''help finish things or go over them to be sure everything is just right when it's presented for sale.''

It is the polishing that is ''the most time-consuming part of the operation,'' Pete explains. Not polishing in the layman's sense of the word, but polishing to remove what is called ''fire scale'' after a piece is completed. ''Jewelry was easy to finish, to polish,'' Pete goes on, ''because you could use a polishing machine,'' but the miniature pieces must be hand-polished. ''It's tedious because you have to be careful not to destroy any of the detail work while

Some Acquisto silver, such as the turkey platter shown at lower left, is made in limited editions. Often Pete's regular collectors will request each of these pieces as they become available, without regard for what he might decide to make next. Shown with the turkey platter are a vegetable bowl and wine cooler to complete the serving of an elegant Thanksgiving meal. Pictured at left are a tea pot, coffee pot. sugar bowl, creamer, and a lion cup.

butts up against the hole in the mold created by the sprue.''

Pete buys his silver in the form of ''grain,'' ''It's like little BB's,'' he explains. He uses a simple mathematical formula to calculate the amount of silver needed before he begins the melting process. ''You have to know exactly how much silver you'll need,'' he cautions, ''so it doesn't overflow or underfill. You melt the silver with a torch, stirring it with a carbon rod to take the air out of it so you don't wind up with air bubbles in the piece, and when the silver looks just right, you turn on the machine. It starts spinning and throws the molten silver into the mold.''

you're polishing it,'' Pete explains. ''Some of the detail work you can't even touch or you will ruin it. And I'm 'picky', too,'' Pete laughs. ''I've had several people I've trained who decided they didn't like working for me because I want it just exactly right.''

Pete's high standards of quality begin with the model, the master, which he creates himself. From one of his collection of books full of photographs and descriptions, he will choose a piece that ''appeals to me, or to Dee, or to both of us,'' he relates, and draft a measured drawing in full-size. He has this drawing reduced to the size the miniature will be, ''and then I just start it,'' Pete says simply.

The original model is created out of brass or tin, usually, Pete explains, ''because they are easy to work with and make a good, clean model with a smooth finish. Sometimes I use silver, but usually I use the softer metals.'' The design is more often ornate than simple ''because it appeals

to me personally,'' Pete explains. ''They are harder to do, but I like the way they look, and I'd rather work on something I like than something I don't.''

Once the model is complete, a stem called a sprue is attached. This will eventually allow the molten silver to flow into the piece. The next step is to create a rubber mold of the piece by encasing it in sheets of rubber in a frame, clamping the mold frame together, and then heating it. ''This is called 'vulcanizing,' '' Pete continues, and it produces a solid block of rubber which must then be carefully cut open to remove the model, leaving an impression of it in the center.

Pete then uses this mold to make a wax impression of the piece. Once that is done and has cooled, ''you have an exact replica of the original piece,'' he explains. This wax pattern is used to make the plaster mold that will eventually be filled with molten silver. ''You put that mold into a centrifugal casting machine,'' he notes, ''with a crucible to hold the silver that

''If you believe in something, you can sell it. If you don't . . .''

The spinning continues until the silver solidifies and the mold becomes ''cherry red on the end,'' Pete continues. ''When it turns black, you dip it in water and the mold disintegrates, and just leaves your silver piece.''

Then the finishing process begins, first with files and rubberized wheels, and finally by hand. Pete always does this part of the finishing process himself, and only turns the final polishing over to his helpers. ''I still do a lot of the polishing,'' he says, but admits, ''I really hate to do that.''

What he does like to do, when there is time, is to be involved in his 14-year-old son Mike's sports career. Proudly pointing out the photographs on the walls of Mike's room, Pete ex-

Seeing this view of the desert outside Albuquerque, it is not difficult to understand why Pete Acquisto loves living where he does.

plains that he has been on all-star teams in baseball, basketball and football. "I coached a lot of these teams but I never get in the picture," Pete remarks ruefully. "I'm always away on a trip." When they are not traveling, Pete and Dee are "always at every game. Sometimes I'll go and watch him practice," he adds.

Pete had been on the wrestling team when he was in high school, always enjoyed physical education, and now plays racquetball for exercise about twice a week when time permits. "I'm never going to be great at it," he confides. "I'm an intermediate player." There is a pool in the backyard of the Acquisto home and Pete explains that "I really like to swim and used to swim a lot when I was young. I was a lifeguard for awhile."

Most of Pete's neighbors in Albuquerque and many of his local friends have no idea what he does for a living.

"I really don't discuss it with them," he admits. "I guess I consider it to be a more public life, and the time at home is more private." As much as he enjoys being at a show and talking with miniatures collectors about his work, "it's also nice to be able to just be 'nobody' when I'm home," he feels.

> *"I've had several people I've trained who decided they didn't like working for me because I want it just exactly right."*

Sometimes Pete thinks about making jewelry again, "but just for fun, not really to get heavily into it," he insists. "I would probably try to do something different in design, and not worry about whether someone wanted it or not."

In the meantime, miniatures present the sort of challenge Pete really enjoys. There are dozens, maybe

hundreds, of designs still to do, pieces that he and Dee have seen in the museums they have visited all over the country. "I've become more interested in the silver service pieces," Pete explains, "and how they were really made originally, what they look like in real life. You get a better idea of that if you can see it in person. Sometimes it's hard to tell the size of something from a picture, even if the dimensions are given."

Besides his huge following of collectors all over the country, Pete takes pride in the recognition he has received from his peers. He was made an I.G.M.A. Fellow in 1984, and two years later was inducted into N.A.M.E.'s Academy of Honor. His standing as an excellent miniatures artisan is something he takes neither lightly nor for granted. "I've tried to establish a reputation for quality and dependability," Pete insists, "and it's worked out pretty well."

One hundred years from now, will his name be as easily recognizable as Paul Revere's is today? It certainly will, if future generations of miniaturists have anything to say about it.

Peter Acquisto at work

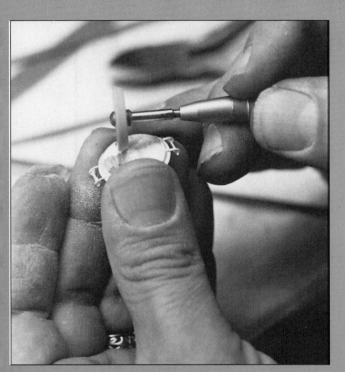

PHOTO 1: Pete is removing a sprue from a cast 1/2'' scale tray. (The sprue is the place where the silver entered the mold.)

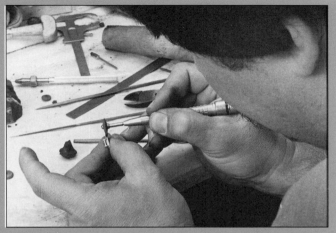

PHOTO 2: Next step of the polishing process is to smooth all over the surface of the tray with a craytex wheel (a rubberized wheel impregnated with grit).

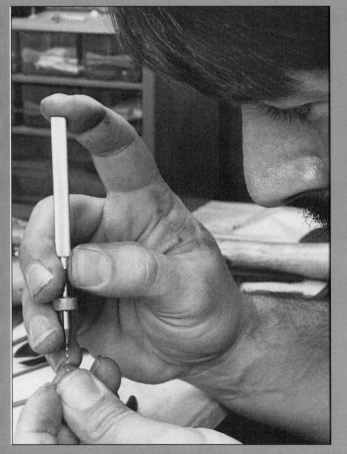

PHOTO 3: Drilling the end of a 1/2'' scale teapot spout.

PHOTO 4: Polishing with a very fine grit polishing point on the side of the limited edition turkey platter.

PHOTO 5: Pete is removing a mold line by filing around the top of the platter cover.

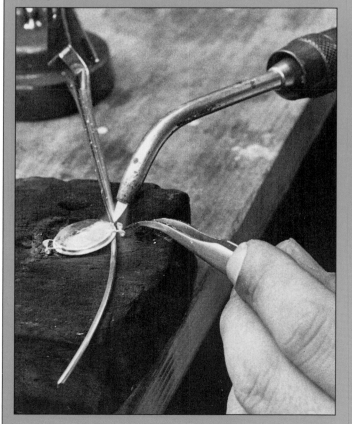

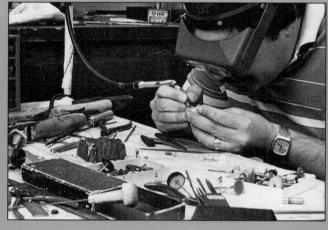

PHOTO 6 (top): He smooths the inside grooves (fluting) with a dental polishing tool used in dentures making.

PHOTO 7 (above): Pete is removing a mold line with a sharp-pointed burr.

PHOTO 8: He is soldering the handle onto a 1/2" scale tray.

PHOTO 9 (above): Using a grinding wheel to shape the basic form of a goblet.

PHOTO 10 (right): Pete is using a graver on the same goblet.

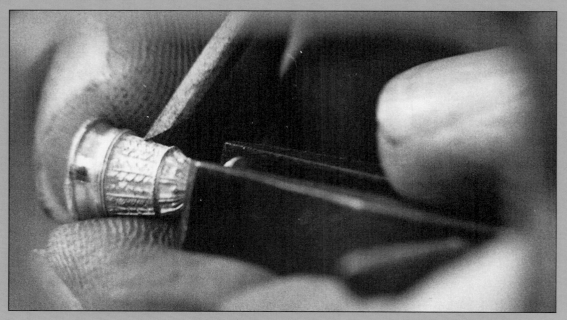

PHOTO 11: In this photo, shot through a magnifying lens, he is cleaning a fancy goblet, removing flashing with a graver.

Marjorie Adams

This world is but a canvas to our imaginations.
—*Henry David Thoreau*

*L*ate at night, while most of us are asleep, the Old Masters are coming to life on a miniature canvas. They are among Marjorie Adams' favorite companions in the quiet hours of the night. She has studied their techniques; she appreciates their genius. She recreates their work precisely on a very small scale.

"I have the privilege of choosing what I like to paint," Marjorie admits, "and I paint what I like." There are portraits and landscapes, in oil and in watercolor. The range of her subjects is ever-widening. Her expertise in reproducing miniature art is undeniable, and she has had a lifelong fascination with fine art. But her career has taken several different paths.

"When I was in college, I had the idea that I'd like to be a dress designer," Marjorie recalls, "but I soon realized that wasn't for me."

A versatile craftsperson, Marjorie built the lace-making stand shown above in a woodworking class, where she learned to rout and bend wood. She also turned the bobbins she uses on a lathe. A small bookmark is the work in progress. Pictured above right are three of the carefully researched and adapted fans, which, along with her paintings, are prized among miniatures collectors. The paintings shown at right were taken from a favorite book of fairy tales that she and her sister had as children.

She attended Ohio Wesleyan University in Delaware, Ohio, where her father was a professor. "Kids got tuition free," she explains simply, "so, of course, we went. Both my sister and I graduated from Ohio Wesleyan." Marjorie received a Bachelor of Arts Degree with a Fine Art major. Except for a few months after she was born in Madison, Wisconsin, she spent all her growing up years in a large, Victorian house in the college community of Delaware.

Marjorie met her future husband, Bob Adams, while both were in college, and they were married several months after graduation. Together they raised a daughter and three sons. But it was wartime when they were married and Bob joined the Navy. Marjorie went to Niagara Falls to live with his parents. "I had a job at Bell Aircraft," she recalls, "doing the original drawings for maintenance manuals. I really enjoyed that. I

worked from blueprints, and sometimes I went down and did the drawings from the plane itself."

After World War II was over, Bob joined Ansco, a film manufacturer in Binghamton, New York, where he worked on quality control. "Then, about 1958 I think, they had a reorganization," Marjorie remembers, "and eliminated about one-third of their employees. Bob lost his job," and the family, by now four of them, moved back to Niagara Falls where, Marjorie continues, "Bob had the idea of starting a photographic business of his own."

Bob also went back to school to work on an engineering degree and "I started a cloth doll business in order

to help the family while he was in school," Marjorie explains. Her 18-inch cloth dolls were distributed by Creative Playthings, a New Jersey-based supplier of educational toys and teaching aids. The dolls were designed to help train kindergarten-age children to dress themselves, "so they had to meet certain specifications and requirements," Marjorie continues.

Once the photography business started to become successful, Marjorie joined her husband in that business. "We had a store downtown," which she managed, "but he did his processing at home," she recalls. When a cab driver stopped by one day and asked if she took identification photos for tax licenses, "I thought, why not?" Marjorie laughs, "and started experimenting, and next thing you know, I was in the portrait business."

The family added a storeroom and studio to their home, consolidated the business, "and for the next fifteen years," Marjorie relates, "I was a photographer." Weddings and baby photographs were the staples of their business. "I'd go to the hospital and take the baby pictures," Marjorie reminisces. "I figure I've probably done over 5,000 babies between the ages of four hours and two days old. It was fascinating."

But by then the marriage had become strained. With three of the children on their own, Marjorie and her youngest son, David, moved to separate quarters, and Marjorie went to work at a frame shop. She also encountered miniatures for the first time.

A friend in the craft group Marjorie belonged to had become interested in miniatures and urged Marjorie to go to a meeting with her. On the way, Marjorie's friend showed her some tiny paintings she had acquired. "I looked at them and thought, I could do better," Marjorie recalls, laughing. "How often have you heard that story? Anyway, I came home and tried a little picture of "Blue Boy," and showed it to her. She told me it was the best painting she had ever seen," Marjorie remembers, pleased.

> *"I'm a sucker when it comes to books. I get books on the various artists and study their styles, study how they did it, their techniques."*

Marjorie loved doing the tiny paintings and was planning to do more of them when her sister telephoned from Ohio. "She said," Marjorie recalls, " 'I think our folks are ready for someone to take care of them.' We had felt," she explains, "that as long as they could manage, the two of them together, we'd leave them alone." Marjorie and her son "both decided this was the thing we had to do, so we went to Delaware and took care of them." Marjorie worked during the day as the office manager at the Delaware Speech and Hearing Center, took care of her parents and the house, and painted at night, sometimes until 2 a.m., establishing a habit she continues today.

She also located an active miniatures group not far away in Columbus and went to her first meeting in the late 70's. "I got nerve enough to show the two paintings I had at the time." Marjorie recalls, "and they liked them." One of the members owned a shop and agreed to take Marjorie's work to sell. "I went home and painted three more, took them up to her, and by the next week she had sold them," Marjorie reminisces. "I was hooked."

This relationship continued until 1981 "when I started doing shows," Marjorie explains, and then "it soon got to the point where I couldn't paint enough for the shows, let alone for her." By then Marjorie was alone; her parents had died. She and her

sister, Dorothy Crane, who was planning to retire soon, decided to move to an old farmhouse Dorothy owned in Washington Courthouse, Ohio.

The house needed extensive renovation and they chose a local contractor to do the work. But before the work could start, foundation damage was discovered, and Marjorie recalls, "He said the best thing to do would be to take it down and start over," so they did. "The reason we chose Charlie in the first place," she reminisces, "was because he said I could help with the work. I had always wanted to build a house."

In the summer of 1981, in her early 60's, Marjorie got her wish. She moved onto the property, living at first in a tent and then in a small house trailer, designed an energy-efficient solar house, and helped with the actual building of it. There was usable lumber from the house they had taken down, "so I spent the first three, solid weeks just taking nails out of lumber," she recalls.

To design the house, Marjorie comments, "I read all the solar books I could get my hands on. The greenhouse is part of our heating system." A door and window in each adjacent room opens to the greenhouse. During the first full year, "I figure it cost us about $157 to heat the house for the entire year," she declares. There are ten-inch thick exterior walls and plenty of insulation.

The rooms she and Dorothy use the most are nearest the greenhouse end, Marjorie points out. Then there are the bedrooms and baths, and at the far end of the house, Marjorie's workshop and a garage. She has a variety of full-size tools such as the radial arm saw she bought while she lived in Delaware. Then when she left her job there, "they gave me a gift certificate," Marjorie recalls, "and I bought the Craftsman band saw." While the house was being built, she had a chance to try Charlie's table

A portion of Marjorie's book collection, which is used for reference and research, is shown on the opposite page. Even her work as a volunteer dispatcher for the Fayette County Life Squad (left) is not unrelated to miniatures, as she frequently works on her paintings or fans while on duty nights and weekends. Her miniature reproduction of Gainsborough's "Blue Boy," and two paintings from Oriental prints are shown above left and above.

saw, "and I didn't think I could live without one," she laughs, "so I bought one."

Her woodworking ability has improved, Marjorie continues, since "I finally took a course in cabinetmaking. I made a list of all the different things I wanted to learn," and used those new skills to make the full-size table she uses for lace making, a craft she first learned in college. The table is kept in the den where she also does her painting.

Every available inch of wall space in this room is filled with bookshelves. There are new books and old books. Some, Marjorie points out, "the how-to-books I've had a long time. I'm a sucker when it comes to books," she laughs. "I get books on the various artists and study their styles, study how they did it, their techniques." One reason, Marjorie claims, "that I have so many books here is that I try to get the best reproduction I can." Citing "Blue Boy" as an example,

she continues, "I had three pictures of him in my files," each with a different-colored background. "So when I went to California, I made a specific point of going to the Huntington to see that picture.

Marjorie travels all over the country to miniature shows, often allowing time in her schedule for visits to museums and to paint along the way. The next time she goes to California, she notes, "I'm going to make it a painting holiday. On the way back, I'm going to mosey across the country and just paint." Her van is equipped for camping, "and I like to drive. I like to see the country," Marjorie insists. "I don't like flying." In the first sixteen months she owned it, Marjorie drove the van 40,000 miles.

When she is at home in Washington Courthouse, there is hardly a moment Marjorie is not busy. There are still projects to complete around the house. She works on her miniature

paintings and fans. And she has a responsible volunteer position with the county's rescue department.

"When I moved down here, I saw a notice in the paper saying they wanted dispatchers," Marjorie recalls. "I said, I'd really like to do that. So I went down and took the course, and now I'm a volunteer dispatcher." The Fayette County Life Squad has five vehicles, she continues, "three here in town. We have an on-base crew all the time. You sleep at night. I am on duty regularly Tuesday and Wednesday nights, from 11:00 p.m. until 8:00 in the morning. Then we're supposed to volunteer at least once a month. I usually do that oftener for weekends because that is all-volunteer time," she explains. In the months that she does not travel a great deal to shows, Marjorie might work from 70 to over 100 hours as a dispatcher.

It is this dedication that earned her the engraved plaque hanging on the

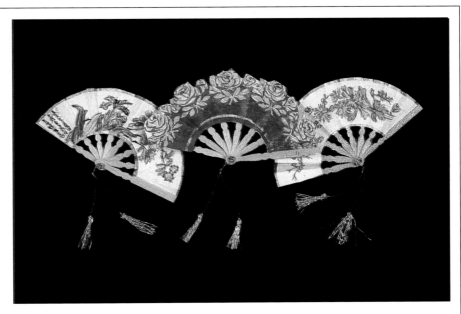

Marjorie's versatility as an artist is evident in the fact that she is as much at home painting original pieces as she is reproducing the work of the Old Masters. Of the four paintings pictured on the opposite page, the two on the left are reproductions: "Landscape with Cattle" by George Henry Durrie (upper left) and "The Avenue, Middelharnis" by Meindert Hobbema (lower left). The seascape at upper right, opposite page, is a Marjorie Adams original, while the zebra painting below it was done for a customer who brought her a full-size print of the Stubbs painting and asked her to copy it. The fans shown at right are all adaptations, drawn from old paintings or antique fans.

wall in her den. It reads: "1986 Richard Snyder Memorial Service Award presented to Marge Adams by the Board of Directors for her dedication and service to the ideals and purpose of the Fayette County Life Squad." It is an award she is very proud of. "I was really thrilled," she smiles.

"One reason I like the night shift," Marjorie explains, "is that I can take my work in, and I do work down there." The rest of the crew might "look over my shoulder," she adds, "and ask, what are you working on today." It is the watercolors she usually paints during quiet moments. "I don't dare take the oil paintings because when that emergency number rings, I'd be afraid I would smear it or something. But, I do a lot of watercolor work down there."

> *"You know, it's funny; it seems like everything you've done in your life leads up to one thing, and this is it."*

The oil paintings are created at her desk at home where there are two lights set up nearby, one incandescent and one fluorescent. One or the other alone would not work, Marjorie explains, "because you have to balance the light. At first, I'd work at night and the next morning my colors looked terrible, so I soon learned that I had to color-balance the light. And I do a lot of my work at night. Dorothy and I are both 'night owls'," Marjorie observes.

"Since Dorothy is retired, and I don't have to punch a time clock," she goes on, "we can keep our own hours. I like classical music and you get the best music at night. So I frequently turn on the radio and get going. I work in the daytime, too," she continues, "but I get going and then look at the clock and it's midnight. I think, I should really get to bed, but the next thing you know, it's two a.m."

During the day Marjorie might be preparing her canvases "exactly the way real, quality canvases are made, but they are a much heavier grade of linen, of course," she notes. Or she might be working on the frames for her paintings which she makes herself. She learned both of these skills when she worked at the frame shop in Niagara Falls, except that they are now done in miniature. "You know, it's funny," she muses, "it seems like everything you've done in your life leads up to one thing, and this is it."

Sometimes it might be her curiosity that sets Marjorie off in a new direction. "People ask me what started me making fans," she points out, "and I can't remember. I don't know where I got the idea, but I just wondered it I could make them, and

tried." She keeps the first one she ever made as an example to show beginning craftsmen so they will not become discouraged. It makes a vivid comparison with the work she does now.

The fan leaf, or mount as it is also called, is made of very thin, imported paper similar to rice paper. Marjorie paints the design with watercolors. The sticks, at least eight and sometimes as many as sixteen, are cut from hardwoods such as maple or cherry. "It has to have practically no grain," Marjorie has found. She uses a precision drill to make the tiny holes in each stick and #34 wire, "the finest wire I can find," she cautions. "You can't even put a needle through the hole, it is so fine."

When the time comes to put each fan together, Marjorie continues, "I finally decided my fingers were my best tools. I can't tell you how many jigs I tried." It is a painstaking process altogether, but one she is willing to share. Marjorie was made a Fellow in I.G.M.A. several years ago, and plans to teach a class in the making of fans at I.G.M.A.'s annual summer school.

Sharing the how-to and talking about miniatures in general is something Marjorie enjoys. "I've gotten into speaking to different groups on miniatures," she comments. "I was asked to speak to a luncheon group here in town, and someone heard that and thought it was a good idea for another group, and then I was asked

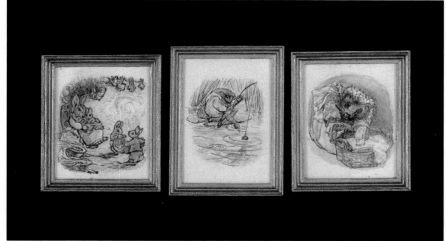

Marjorie draws upon the Old Masters, book illustrations and her own surroundings as sources of inspiration for her miniature paintings. Pictured above is Marjorie's miniature reproduction of Gainsborough's famous painting, "Mrs. Chamberlayne." At upper right are three of her popular Beatrix Potter pictures. The two floral paintings at right are originals, copied from plants belonging to her sister, Dorothy. The plant on the left in the photo is an Oriental cactus; on the right are aurelian lilies.

to speak at one of the groups at our church," she continues. She also put some of her work into a local, juried art show. "That was the first time I've ever put work out in exhibit," she admits.

One of Marjorie's miniature paintings in that show was called "Friends," an original, not a reproduction. It was done from a black and white snapshot of her son David as a boy, holding a rabbit, "a picture that I've liked for a long time," Marjorie notes. "I just decided I'd do it." When the show's judge critiqued the first place winners, he included Marjorie's painting to talk about. "It was a second place winner," she remembers, "but he was so impressed with it, he just had to talk about it. He commented on the quality of the painting for its size, and he liked the way it was painted."

When Marjorie began painting in miniature, "I decided the way to become established, first, was by doing reproductions. After I did that, I started making my own," she continues. The originals are displayed along with the reproductions; often they look similar enough to prompt the comment: "Adams, I don't know the artist," which Marjorie has been amused to hear at shows. "Anything that has 'Adams' on it is my own original work," she smiles.

Each of Marjorie's paintings has a certain amount of information on the back, including her signature and the date it was completed. She also puts a number to indicate how many times she has done that particular painting, the title of the work, and the artist's name. It is secondary information that she feels her collectors should have. Of primary importance, though, is

what is on the front of each canvas.

"When you look at art work," Marjorie feels, "there is just something about a picture that you like. There's an impact, or a feeling. You just build a rapport with that picture. It's fun," she continues. "This whole thing is fun. The people you meet are such delightful people, the imaginative kind. They're all creative. I love doing the painting. Of course, I could do other painting," but, she adds smiling, "I don't think I'll ever get out of miniatures because the people are just wonderful."

With her unabashed enthusiasm for her work and for the people she has come to know in the world of miniatures, the Old Masters Marjorie Adams carefully creates will be coming to life on a miniature canvas for a long time to come.

Marjorie Adams at work

PHOTO 1: An overall view of Marjorie's painting work area.

PHOTO 2: Marjorie is working on a portrait by copying a photo provided by a customer.

PHOTO 3 (left): A close-up view of the photograph, with Marjorie's unfinished portrait shown through a magnifier.

PHOTO 4 (above): She is painting a picture from a print of the painting, "The Milk Carrier," by William Shayer.

PHOTO 5: A close-up of the print, and Marjorie's painting.

PHOTO 6: An originial painting, shown large and in miniature.

PHOTO 7: Painting a fan leaf.

PHOTO 8: Mounting a fan leaf onto assembled sticks.

PHOTO 9: Final touches of gold are added to a reproduction of a fan shown in the 1984 Smithsonian exhibit, ''Fanfare.''

PHOTO 10: Marking the length of wood needed for a frame.

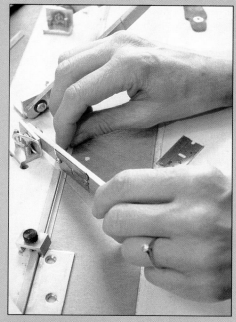

PHOTO 11: Cutting a piece of frame wood.

PHOTO 12: Gluing the frame pieces together.

PHOTO 13 (left): Checking the measurements on a finished glued frame. Each side has to match the opposite side in length exactly.

PHOTO 14 (above): Cutting the design on a carved frame piece.

PHOTO 15 (left): Fitting the painting into the frame.

Charles & Ferbie Claudon

*Artistic growth is, more than it is anything else, a refining
of the sense of truthfulness.*

—*Willa Cather*

Might he have been a Renaissance artist? Could she have been a Bolivian pianist? A fortune teller suggested both possibilities to Charles and Ferbie Claudon when they were first married in 1969. She also told them they had been married to each other before, in an earlier life, probably in late-1800's Germany.

Although some of us might disbelieve such suggestions, there is no denying the fact that this pair has a perfect meshing of creativity, talent and interests in their present life. "Every hobby that we've ever taken up deals with creativity," Chuck observes, sitting in the studio of the couple's Park Forest, Illinois home, surrounded by the evidence of their talents and interests.

Chuck was born in Illinois in 1943, grew up there, and matriculated at Illinois State University where he received his Bachelor's Degree in Speech and Drama in 1966. "I trained from the beginning as a director," he explains. "I don't think I ever had in

mind that I would go into the theater in any other aspect.'' He had worked in summer stock during his college years and decided, ''I didn't really like the kind of life one has to lead in the theater. But, I liked what the theater did. I liked presenting something and having the feedback from it,'' the response from an audience.

''I knew I could do that through teaching,'' Chuck continues, so he began a career in education in the Decatur, Illinois high school, teaching English and working as the school's drama coach. His students presented three plays each school year; Chuck directed them and designed the costumes and sets.

During his college years, one of Chuck's favorite courses had been set design. ''I think the visual aspects of the theater are what really fascinated me throughout,'' he says now. As part of that course, Chuck built his first miniature setting, a half-inch-scale model for the play, *Desire Under the Elms*. The model, a four-room, New England saltbox house,

''High Cream'' (top) was completed in 1984 and illustrates a day nursery with a little girl asleep on a couch and four cats having high tea — or rather, high cream. ''The purpose was to show how cats can be utilized in a setting,'' Chuck explains. ''Catfish'' (above) is a delightful example of Chuck's imaginative approach to his sculpture.

was built of illustration board and illuminated with tiny, Italian Christmas tree lights.

Although he was not required to do so in order to complete this course, Chuck built a total of eight half-scale

models of various stage settings over the next few weeks. Drawings of the sets would have sufficed, but Chuck believes ''models are much more impressive.'' He used this technique with the first school play he directed in Decatur. ''I would do scale models of the sets to show the students what each set was going to look like,'' Chuck explains. He also showed the scale models to a colleague in the English Department who had offered to help sew the costumes, and who would become Chuck's wife shortly thereafter.

Kentucky-born Ferbie Fox was brought up in a small town where she learned about fabrics and costume at a very young age. ''My mother was a seamstress,'' she explains, ''one of two in the town, and she sewed all day long, every day. She did everything, from coats to slipcovers.'' With her mother to instruct her, Ferbie notes, ''I started making doll clothes when I was two years old.'' When Chuck and Ferbie were first married, she created much of their wardrobe. ''I made all of Chuck's suits,'' she

Chuck and Ferbie Claudon, whose accomplishments represent a meshing of interests and talents, are shown in their studio (above), researching a new collaboration. Every detail is carefully plotted. "What do you think of these fabrics?" Ferbie asks Chuck. Chuck designed this attractive studio (right) which the Claudons added to their home. The shelves along one wall hold both their book collection and several room settings. The flat surface in the rear has storage below and is at a comfortable working height from the floor. The studio is almost always kept as neat as it looks here because, they have found, they cannot leave any work in progress where the two cats might get into it. "Everything has to be put in a safe place," Ferbie points out, "or they'd have it on the floor."

continues, "and all my suits, coats, everything."

Ferbie earned her Bachelor's Degree in English at Murray State University in Kentucky, taught a year at the junior high in her hometown, and then took a job at Decatur's MacArthur High School where she and Chuck met.

The Claudons were married in October 1969, moved to Park Forest where they still live, and Chuck became an English teacher and head of the drama program at the high school nearby. Ferbie switched then from full-time to substitute teaching, and agreed to be responsible for the drama department's costumes. "They were really getting two of us for the price of one," she insists, practically.

"The first year we were here we did a Shakespearean play," Ferbie remembers. There were forty students to be outfitted, "from the skin out, and there was nothing in the stockroom except one huge bolt of blue fabric which we never used," she laughs. In only six weeks, Ferbie, with very little help, created Eliza-

bethan garb for the forty cast members, some of whom needed more than one costume. It is a credit to her sewing skills that some of the costumes were still in wearable condition when she and Chuck retired from school theater work in 1986, almost 17 years after they were originally made.

When Chuck and Ferbie settled into their home in Park Forest, they had access to furnishings that had been in Chuck's family for years. "My family is a family of packrats," Chuck insists, "and my grandmother, who had recently died, had kept everything in the house." Chuck and Ferbie were able to choose the pieces they wanted to furnish their new home, including

even a mantelpiece, "although we don't have a fireplace," Chuck points out, because they both liked it.

Park Forest, a suburb of Chicago, is a planned community built in 1948. "This house is like all the other ranch-style houses in Park Forest," Chuck notes, as he conducts a tour of their home, until visitors enter the addition constructed a few years ago to provide a studio and more storage space.

"I designed it and did a floor plan for it," Chuck says proudly, "and the contractor made no changes in the floor plan at all." Cupboards and bookshelves line two walls, and there is a wide ledge built in along the back wall, with drawer space below, which

The distinctly feline quality of all Chuck's cats, both realistic and whimsical, is widely recognized among collectors. Some credit for their lifelike attributes must be given to Chuck's live-in models, who provide him with endless poses and antics to sculpt. China Silk (top), one of the two cats in residence, likes to sit in the top of one of Ferbie's rolling carts full of supplies. The other Claudon cat, Katie Scarlett (above), catnaps on a cushion where Chuck will later retrieve her shed hairs to use as whiskers for his sculpted cats. The dollhouse shown at right was begun by Chuck in 1969. Built into two bookcases, it sits against a wall in the entry foyer of the Claudons' home and incorporates many details Chuck has since used in individual room settings, as well as the work of other miniatures artisans.

serves as Chuck's workbench. A comfortable couch faces the bay window overlooking a back yard full of birds.

"We debated about a fireplace versus the window," Chuck comments, "and part of the reason we originally bought this house was because it backs up on an area that will never be built on, so this is one of the nicest back yards in the entire town. We figured the window was much more important."

The padded window seat is a favorite bird-watching spot for the Claudons' two cats, China Silk and Katie Scarlett. It is these two, as well as Button, 17 years old when she died last year, who are the models for

Chuck's sculpted cats.

Although there are now 14 realistic poses, Chuck insists that the first cat he sculpted "looked like a meatloaf,"

> *"The moment you break free is when you decide: this is what I do. It is the moment that art actually begins."*

and adds, "I'm still learning sculpting. I'm self-taught and I surprise myself every time I sculpt a cat that I like." Once each original cat has been

sculpted, it is sent to a caster who also works with several other miniatures artisans. The resulting cast epoxy is "very rigid," Chuck explains, "plus you can cut them and put them in different positions. We just use epoxy to put them back together." Chuck handpaints each cat and adds the whiskers, using real cat fur.

It is the ability to change a cat's position that led to the collection of "Kitty Kitsch" Chuck and Ferbie create together, using Button as the original model. "She had a very, very strong personality," Ferbie insists. "She was crazy about us, and she idolized Chuck, but she didn't like anybody else." Button's strong per-

sonality, "so demanding and haughty," Ferbie smiles, "inspired a lot of those dressed cats."

Chuck and Ferbie's collaboration on the dressed cats was a logical continuation of her life-long hobby, collecting, creating, and dressing dolls. Her parents had started her doll collection when she was very young, and Ferbie has continued to make and dress dolls whenever she has had the time. The collection now numbers about 80. The largest is a soft-sculpture lady named "Gertrude" who is almost full-size and sits in a rocker in the Claudons' living room. "Our house sitter when we are away," Chuck points out with a smile.

Ferbie became interested in doing costume dolls when she was working on the full-size costumes for that first Shakespearean school play. "At the beginning," Chuck recalls, "Ferbie sewed a great deal, but didn't like to sew without patterns. So when we started doing Shakespeare, I would draft the patterns from any books we could find. Now," he continues, "she does everything without a pattern."

It was excellent training for the

"I'm very interested in the Edwardian period," Chuck admits. "I like the designs of the period; I like the Arts and Crafts Movement. This room setting (above) is called "April 1912." Pictured at right is an example of Ferbie's work, a grandmother and baby which she sculpted and dressed.

work she does now, Ferbie believes, "because it's all a matter of knowing the shape of the garment, knowing how it's put together, and then knowing how to get the same effect on a smaller scale." Ferbie works both in one-inch scale and in half-inch, which she prefers over any other. The "Kitty Kitsch" collection is half-inch, as is the collection of figures Ferbie sculpts and dresses herself.

There are perhaps a dozen different poses, but since they are also made of cast epoxy, their parts can be rearranged, a head turned, an arm raised, and the figure put back together again. Ferbie refers to them as "figures" rather than dolls because her focus is the clothing they are wearing, and the reality of the figure's position. "I'm not concerned with the figure itself," she com-

ments. Instead, she strives to make the costuming "as accurate, historically, as it can be in that scale."

Although her favorite scale is half-inch, Ferbie and Chuck collaborate often in both half-inch and one-inch scale. Chuck's first miniature settings were the set designs he did in half-inch. Then when he and Ferbie were first married, he started a dollhouse in one-inch scale, built into two book-

Chuck enjoys working on Egyptian room settings as an occasional change of pace. He spent an entire summer painting "Malkata, 1453 B.C." (top), a reproduction of King Tut's bedroom. "I really do like painting," he confesses, "as much as anything else in the process." A sculpted cat, his first realistic one, is in this room. Two more examples of Claudon cats are shown above.

cases that are displayed in the Claudons' entry hall. "It was designed to be 1912, but it is fairly eclectic," Chuck observes, and filled with the things they both have collected, as well as items Chuck has made.

When Chuck decided to replace the

original needlepoint rugs in the dollhouse, Ferbie created purses out of them for herself and both their mothers. The figures appearing in many of the rooms are by Cecil Boyd, "the first figures I found that I really liked the scale of," Chuck explains. And many of the interior details have since evolved into individual rooms.

Chuck created his first one-inch scale room setting in 1975, and has completed over a dozen since then. "We start out wanting to do things like everybody else," Chuck feels. "The moment you break free is when you decide: this is what I do. It is the moment that art actually begins."

Like theater sets, the rooms are designed to bring the viewer into the scene. Noting their similarity and recalling his earlier training in set design, Chuck feels, "One doesn't really change." Each of the rooms, too, has required an extensive amount of research, a labor of love as far as Chuck is concerned.

"That is one of the things I get the most enjoyment from," he insists, recalling the work he prepared for his Master's Degree in Drama from the University of Illinois in 1971. It is a

compilation of one hundred years of furniture and costume design, from 1870 to 1970, and a book he refers to often. It encompasses the Edwardian period, of course, one of Chuck's favorite periods. "I like the designs for that period," he says. "I like the

> *"...it's all a matter of knowing the shape of the garment, knowing how it's put together, and then knowing how to get the same effect on a smaller scale."*

Arts and Crafts Movement, Art Deco," and for total contrast, Egyptian.

Chuck completed his first Egyptian room, "Malkata, 1453 B.C." in 1978. It is a reproduction of King Tut's bedroom, and in its design is typical of many of Chuck's rooms. "I start with a room that will be true to scale and true to angles," he explains, "and then I begin cutting sections, distorting for sight lines, to get the angles I want.''

Since he builds interior walls from illustration board, this technique works very well. ''The angle is correct visually, but there is always some slight distortion,'' he continues, adding that ''this room showed me what I really enjoy doing, and that is the painting.'' Once the research was completed, and the design for the interior decoration laid out on graph paper, Chuck spent most of an entire summer painting the Egyptian room. ''We laugh about the fact that the summer I did this room, Ferbie decided the outside of the house needed painting,'' Chuck confides. ''So she painted outside and I painted this. She had her summer project and I had mine.''

Even though they occasionally work on separate projects, when they are working together their differing philosophies complement each other. ''You're designing the set for the person,'' Ferbie reminds Chuck. ''My main interest is the person that goes into it, so we're looking at it from two different angles.'' Together, though, Chuck feels, ''we think 'periods' with almost everything.''

It is a thought process that has

> ''I'm self-taught and I surprise myself every time I sculpt a cat I like.''

become second nature to both of them, and serves them well in their research. Both Chuck and Ferbie are museum-goers, in Chicago where they are members of the Art Institute, as well as in other cities they visit. ''We enjoy the portrait museums,'' Ferbie comments. ''It's interesting to see the techniques and to see if they can be adapted, if there is anything we can use.'' They both look at fabrics, accessories, ideas for costumes, ''the way the figures are rendered,'' Chuck adds, ''the poses and sometimes ideas for cats, as people.''

Ideas are often filed away in a memory bank for future use. ''Some

Cats by Chuck include ''Button Goes to Grandma's'' (above), ''America's Founding Felines''(right), and a vase of ''cat tails'' (lower right) getting the once-over from a cat that still has its own.

of our inspiration just sort of rattles around for awhile,'' Chuck laughs. ''We have it up here,'' he says, tapping his forehead, ''think about it, and then a year from now it'll suddenly jump back.''

In a more practical vein, Ferbie says, ''I'll usually keep a notebook. We do most of our deciding on periods or settings when we're driving, even driving around doing errands on a Saturday morning, or on planes coming back from a show.''

They have been exhibiting and selling their work at shows all over the country only for the past half dozen years, although they have been members of N.A.M.E. since 1973. Chuck has served as one of N.A.M.E.'s Regional Coordinators since 1979 and is currently on the N.A.M.E. Board of Directors, they were both elected to the Academy of Honor in 1985, and together they co-chaired the committee presenting the 1986 N.A.M.E. National Houseparty in Chicago. Chuck and Ferbie are also I.G.M.A. artisans.

It was a fellow miniaturist who suggested the name for their business, The Butterfly Cat Studio. ''When we were not yet a business, but knew that we were going to be doing cats,''

*"Gertrude" (right), an almost life-size
soft sculpture figure that Ferbie created,
sits in front of the fireplace surround and
mantle that was originally in Chuck's
grandmother's home. When "Gertrude"
is not reading a book, one of the
Claudons' cats might take a nap in her
lap, and she is "a great house sitter when
we are away," Chuck points out. Above,
one of the lifelike felines from the Butterfly
Cat Studio collection licks its paw, while
"Mama Cat" at lower right shows off her
newborn babies.*

Ferbie remembers, "we were talking
with George and Joan Passwaters
about it. Joanie said she had a copy of
the Kewpieville series Rose O'Neill
did for *Ladies Home Journal* in 1924,
about a cat with butterfly wings."
Chuck recalls now that they both
loved the name and realized "it is so
unique that everybody asks about it."
Joan gave them the magazine page
which is now framed and hanging on
the wall in the Claudons' studio where
they can see it every day.

During the school year, weekdays
begin early for Chuck and Ferbie. If
the weather is pleasant, he usually
walks the one mile to school. She
walks with him part way so that they
can spend a little extra time together,
and "to get my day's instructions,"
Ferbie laughs.

Besides teaching a basic English
course, Chuck teaches a two-year
course with another instructor,
"History and Thought of Western
Man." "I teach the English and art,"

SEVEN·HOVRS·TO·WORK·TO·SLVMBER·SEVEN
TO·THE·WORLD·ALLOT·AND·ALL·TO·HEAVEN.

NANA

MICHAEL

JOHN

he explains, "and my colleague teaches music, social studies and history. Very bright kids, very complex ideas. I have a chance to talk about the modern art movements, and what art is. It's a course that keeps me sane," Chuck insists.

While Chuck is at school, Ferbie works at least four days each week on her sculpted figures or at the "Kitty Kitsch" dressed cats. Since they are essentially the same size, her patterns are often interchangeable, and until she began working in half-inch scale, Ferbie sewed almost every part of each costume. "I could not be convinced that gluing would work," she admits now. "All the one-inch scale costumes were sewn, except for the bonnet. That almost had to be glued. When I started half-inch, I had no choice but to use the glue. And I have to say in my own defense," she smiles, "glue is a lot better these days."

Most of the fabrics Ferbie uses are natural fibers such as silks and cottons, "but if there's a particular color I want to use and I can't find anything

that's right," she notes, "I'll use a blend." It is the effect she is trying to communicate that is important to Ferbie. Just as it is to Chuck.

"I look upon what we do as a personal expression," he insists, "a way to communicate our view of life, of the world. We have been discussing Mary Cassatt in the art segment of my course at school," Chuck continues, "and one of the quotes attributed to her is this: 'I learned that acceptance on someone else's terms is worse than rejection.' I tend to agree with her. I think what people see is us, all sorts of aspects of us, our personal viewpoint." A Renaissance artist probably could not have said it any better.

A poignant moment from "Peter Pan" (top): The children have left, transported out the open window on the right, father sleeps in the dog house, and "The Vigil" has begun. Pictured above, left, are two turn-of-the-century women dressed by Ferbie in appropriately documented clothing. Her careful research and talented hands and needle are also evident in the 16th century family shown above.

Chuck and Ferbie Claudon at work

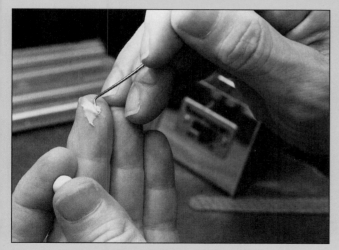

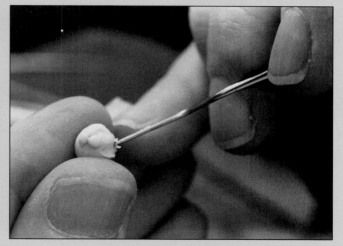

PHOTO 1 (above): Chuck forms a nose for a realistic cat.
*PHOTO 2 (above right): Now he is beginning to shape the jaw
area after having applied the nose and mouth.*

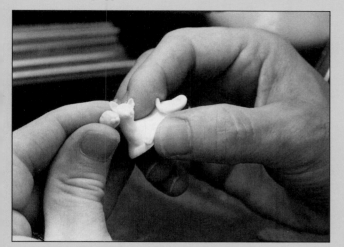

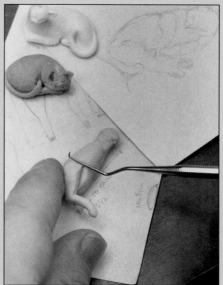

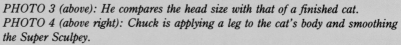

PHOTO 3 (above): He compares the head size with that of a finished cat.
*PHOTO 4 (above right): Chuck is applying a leg to the cat's body and smoothing
the Super Sculpey.*
*PHOTO 5 (left): Shown here are: the cat in the process of being sculpted; a
completed, cast cat (center); a cat sculpted from Super Sculpey and baked (left);
and a set of drawings for checking sizes.*
PHOTO 6 (right): Chuck is working on the paws and arms.

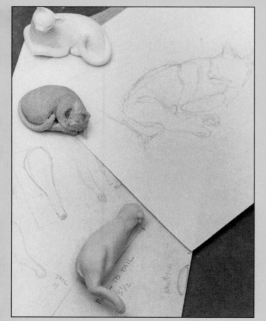

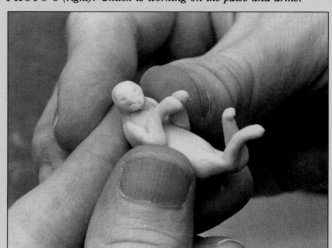

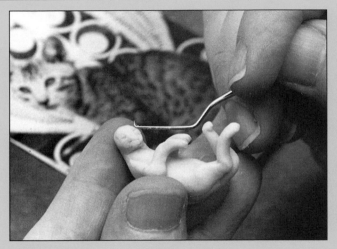

PHOTO 7: Chuck keeps a photo of one of his cats nearby for reference.

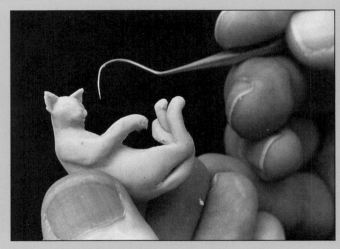

PHOTO 8: Now ears are applied to the kitty's head.

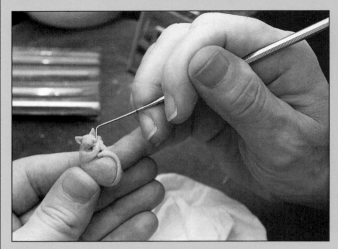

PHOTO 9: After baking, Chuck refines the sculpture by adding more Super Sculpey before baking it one more time.

PHOTO 10: Three steps are shown here with tools and reference materials. The three cats are (from the bottom of the photo): sculpted from Super Sculpey and baked; cast epoxy; and painted.

PHOTO 11 (left) & 12 (above): Two views of Chuck at work in his studio, showing several cats in progress while China Silk watches the procedure with interest.

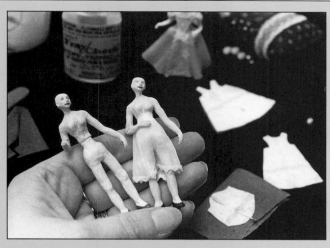

PHOTO 13: *Ferbie holds two painted, epoxy figures. A channel, or ditch, at the waistline eliminates bulkiness of the clothing.*

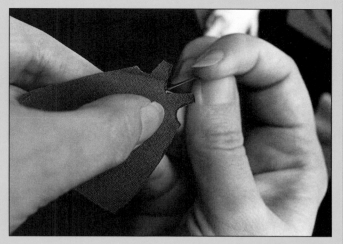

PHOTO 14: *She applies Fray Check to the edges of the fabric to avoid fraying.*

PHOTO 15: *The first step in beginning the costume is to glue it on the doll at the shoulder.*

PHOTO 16: *Ferbie glues on the front part of the garment.*

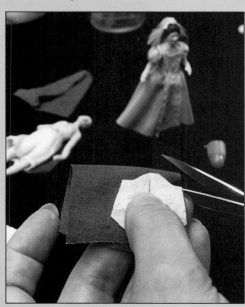

PHOTO 17: *She cuts out the sleeve using the pattern she has made from paper toweling, which she prefers for all her miniature patterns because it is so flexible.*

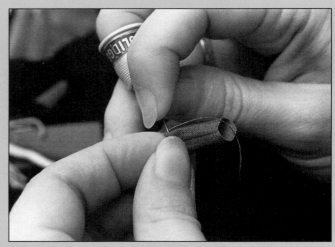

PHOTO 18 (left) & 19 (above): Ferbie glues the sleeve together (the cart to her right is Katie Scarlett's favorite napping spot), and overcasts the sleeve cap.

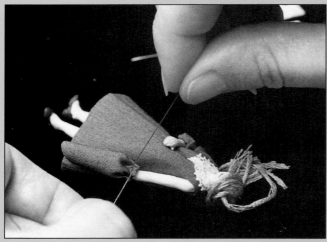

PHOTO 20: She attaches the bottom of the sleeve to the doll's arm.

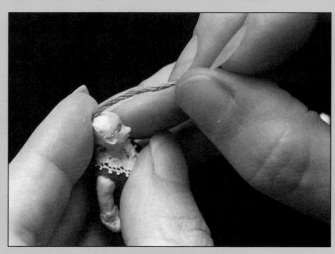

PHOTO 21: The wigging process is begun with embroidery floss right on the doll's body.

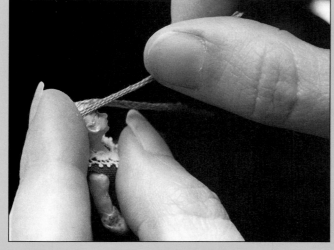

PHOTO 22 (above) & 23 (right): Continuing the wigging, she separates the strands of floss before styling.

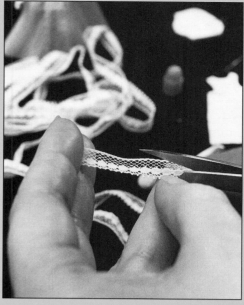

PHOTO 24: The lace is trimmed to correct scale for 1/2''.

PHOTO 25: Ferbie glues the lace collar to the dress.

PHOTO 26 (above): Glue drops applied to the neck simulate pearls. PHOTO 27 (right): Boy and girl dolls, both made from the same mold.

PHOTO 28 (left): 1/2'' scale figures before and after painting.

Sharon Garmize

I broider the world upon a loom,
I broider with dreams my tapestry;...
—*Arthur Symons*

*I*magine the magic carpet in a fairy tale. Its design is timeless; its weave looks as fragile as a spider web. The colors shimmer and glow with a radiance all their own. To be able to create such a treasure is beyond the realm of possibility for most people. But these magical carpets are easily possible in the expert hands of Sharon Garmize.

The ability to create these miniature rugs may well relate in some way to a rich Hungarian heritage. Sharon is a second generation American, born in February 1950, the first of five children, in a small town near Wilkes-Barre, Pennsylvania. Her grandparents emigrated to this country in the early 1900's. "When I was born," Sharon comments, "my parents lived with my father's parents, so I was raised with them." The grandparents had by then established their business, a beer garden, in this coal mining town.

"It's been said that my grandmother was a gypsy," Sharon observes about the person who has most influenced her life. "We are very much alike," she goes on, "character-wise, personality-wise, our likes and dislikes. We even looked a little bit like each other." Anna Berish took Sharon "under her wing. She taught me how to do my first piece of needlework when I was three years old," Sharon relates.

From her grandmother, Sharon learned how to stitch, to do tatting and embroidery, to knit and crochet, to do counted cross stitch and weaving. "My grandmother did everything," Sharon marvels. "She made soap. She made her own clothing and mine. She canned food, raised poultry, and made pillows from the feathers. Almost everything we had, she made. And I'm the only one of five children who has her talents. The others are really not like me at all."

Sharon has another of her grandmother's talents, the ability to see into the future. Although she recalls that people often came to the beer garden to have her grandmother read their palms, Sharon was not aware that she had the same psychic ability until she was 13 and had a dream about her grandmother's death. "And she died," Sharon claims, "exactly the way I dreamed it." Sharon has had many psychic revelations since then. "It's not psychic on command," she insists, "it's when I have a feeling." Of her own life, Sharon says philosophically, "I know good things are going to happen to me, and I know bad things are going to happen to me. But I know exactly where my life is going, and I feel confident that I am going to be okay."

After she graduated from high school at the age of 16, and with an I.Q. of 153, Sharon went off to college at Penn State University, intending to major in art. "I can't draw," she confesses, "but I always did love art and I wanted to learn." She soon found that "art and I weren't getting along," so Sharon switched her major to food service, thinking that she might have a career in hotel and res-

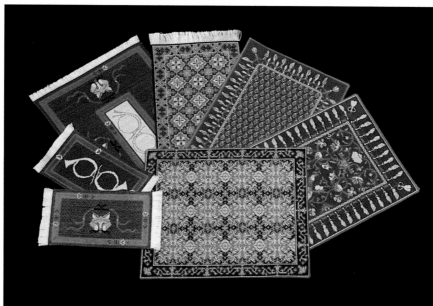

taurant management. She went into retailing instead.

"I started out as a clerical," Sharon remembers, "and within a year I was an assistant buyer. A short time after that, at the age of 21, I was the lingerie buyer," at a Pennsylvania-based department store. Sharon held that job for the next seven years, during which time she met and married her former husband. Their marriage ended in divorce in the summer of 1982.

Sharon recalls seeing the dollhouse a friend had in 1976, "and my ex-husband decided I needed a dollhouse, too," she reminisces. "We went to a

To many collectors, the name "Sharon Garmize" is synonymous with miniature Persian rugs, although Sharon does many other types of needlework which can be found in fine miniature homes around the country. The ideas for her rugs come from a multitude of sources, and not all of them are Persian. Many are from English and French sources as well. In addition, Sharon works exquisite miniature samplers, some of which are shown above on a full-size sampler from her collection. She makes regular forays into the antiques market, in search of needlework and fabrics.

show in Pottstown, Pennsylvania, and bought my dollhouse. My very first miniature was a Christmas tree made out of pipe cleaners. And I was hooked,'' she laughs.

As she began furnishing her house, Sharon found that there was some carpeting available, but decided, ''I could do needlework,'' and found the materials to try her own rugs. ''I had a very difficult time finding supplies,'' she recalls, and the results were discouraging. ''After about 30 minutes of working on it, I said, that's it, never again,'' Sharon confides. But she thought about it again a few months later, found the silk gauze she uses today, and ''I tried it again. And here I am today,'' she states matter-of-factly.

Sharon began exhibiting and selling her rugs at miniature shows in 1979. She remembers well the reaction to her work then. One miniatures artisan told her he didn't like her work because it was ''too fine.'' Another artisan, unknown to Sharon at the time, told her she ''hated'' her.

Sharon found out later that the woman also did miniature needlework. It was a very unsettling introduction to miniatures shows, but Sharon's own rugs were a sell-out at the show, in spite of the adverse comments.

Sharon was made a Fellow in the International Guild of Miniatures Artisans in 1981, and she joined the

American Needlepoint Guild and the Embroidery Guild of America that same year. It was through the American Needlepoint Guild that Sharon heard of an international needlepoint competition to be held in Monaco in May 1982. ''I sent in some photographs of my work, and thought, well, I'll probably never hear anything,'' she remembers. Shortly thereafter Sharon received a letter asking her to exhibit her work in Monaco. "It was the first time I had ever traveled alone," Sharon continues. "I took my carpets with me, and this was the first time they had actually seen my work."

> *"I kept saying to myself, get your act together. You cannot cry in front of Princess Grace."*

Sharon's "five or six carpets plus a tiny 84-mesh firescreen" were assigned number 13 in the exhibit. "My lucky number happens to be 13," Sharon smiles. Still, she thought to herself then, "I will never have a chance with all the competition that is here." The 25 competitors were gathered in the lobby of Monaco's L'Hermitage Hotel to wait while Princess Grace judged the needlework inside. "We had been briefed on the proper etiquette in speaking with her," Sharon remembers, "and were told that the person who was to get the award would be called in."

When the president of the Guild indicated to Sharon that she had won, "I started crying," she recalls. As Sharon walked across the lobby, "I kept saying to myself, get your act together. You cannot cry in front of Princess Grace. I went in there and we had a lovely conversation. She was very beautiful, a very normal person who actually knew the town that I had lived in."

Princess Grace, growing up Grace Kelly in Philadelphia, had gone to summer camp as a child not far from Sharon's hometown. "So she knew all about my town," Sharon continues.

During the four days Sharon was in Monaco she had a tour of the Palace, had a chance to talk with Princess Grace at luncheon, and was delighted to learn that "she was totally impressed with my work," Sharon reminisces. The group was also invited to a demonstration of flower arranging the night before the competition at the Princess Grace Theatre. "I was

really quite fascinated by that," Sharon laughs, "because my idea of arranging flowers was to put a dozen roses in a vase. These were huge flower arrangements, some about eight feet tall."

For the actual competition, the only criteria in the judging was that the work be needlepoint. "No cross stitch, no crewel work, only needlepoint," Sharon points out. Authenticity was not a criteria, although Sharon's work had been researched and documented. "The workmanship, the design, the quality," were what the judges were looking for, Sharon explains. Besides the coveted Princess Grace Award, Sharon also received a red ribbon in the overall competition.

When the exhibit went on to London following the competition in

Monaco and sponsored by the London chapter of the American Needlepoint Guild, Sharon's work won the top prize there. She was presented that award by the wife of the U.S. Ambassador to the United Kingdom.

One of the reasons that Sharon's work is unique as well as award-winning is that each piece is worked without a chart. Sharon copies her miniature needlework directly from the full-size original, or from a photograph of the original. "I have a pretty good library of Persian carpet and antique needlework books," Sharon feels. Many of the books have been published by museums. She also subscribes to auction house catalogs, "Sotheby's and Christie's have beautiful color pictures," she continues, "and are a major source of information for me because they give some

A Sheraton-style sofa in the living room (opposite page, top) is Sharon's favorite place to work. Her companion here is her miniature Schnauser, Batchka, recently the mother of four pups, whose name is a Lithuanian slang word for "barrel" or "fatso." Some of her miniatures work, however, is done seated before her computer, a recent, and indispensable addition to her home (opposite page, below). A charted needlework piece can be seen on the screen. Pictured on this page, above, are some of Sharon's rug designs that are available in half-inch scale in addition to one-inch. The framed jeweled peacock kit shown at right can also be made into a pillow.

history on each rug,'' as well as the size of the piece.

"I go to museums whenever I can,'' Sharon notes, and she shops in the antiques market often, partly because she collects antiques herself and partly to see the antique needlework currently for sale. "As you can see, I enjoy antiques,'' she adds, pointing out the collections in her attractive home in the woods in Mountaintop, Pennsylvania. "I collect old needlework. I am now collecting old lace, and I have recently purchased two antique samplers.'' Her various collections, displayed in her home, also include antique kitchen utensils, old patent medicines, Wedgwood, perfume bottles, and an extensive archive of newspapers and magazines, mostly from the early part of this century and the end of the last. Part of her collection of glass marbles fills a child's antique wagon, which is topped with Plexiglas, and used as a coffee table in the family room.

Sharon's favorite place to work is in the living room, sitting on a Sheraton-style sofa. There is a good light source on the table next to her, but "my eyes don't get tired,'' she insists, even though she may work from seven in the morning until 1:00 or 2:00 a.m. the next. "Going back to my grandmother again,'' Sharon observes, "she still had near perfect vision when she died at the age of 76, and I feel that I inherited her eyesight.'' Commenting that she goes to an optometrist about twice a year who tells her she does not need glass-

Sharon's collection of clay marbles forms the backdrop for a saddlebag (top), made with a fringe knotted in macrame-style. "It's a very hard way to do it, to make it look like it's a mess,'' she believes. Sharon's unerring sense of color is one of the main reasons that her rugs, like the one at left worked in all silk, French thread, are cherished by collectors. The same fine care and craftsmanship are given to pillows, a necessary and common accessory in many miniature settings, that take on a special importance when executed in needlepoint by Sharon Garmize (center left). Since she likes to work on different pieces at different times, Sharon usually has several works in progress (opposite page).

es, Sharon adds, "your eyes are a muscle; it's the best muscle I have in my body," she laughs.

There are usually at least five projects in progress at any given time, and Sharon works on them alternately. "I tend to get bored fairly easily," she admits. "If I'm not in the mood for doing one, I'll work on another." Many of these works in progress are special commissions and one-of-a-kind pieces requested by a collector. Or she might be designing a piece that will eventually be offered in kit form.

> *"Along with scaling down the pattern, it's very important to also scale down the colors."*

If a particular piece of needlepoint is going to become a kit, Sharon will complete the piece and then create a chart for it. She might then work the piece again, using the chart, to double-check its accuracy and workability, but, she admits, "I don't really like to do the same thing twice. I never did like to repeat things."

Most needleworkers, however, do prefer to work from a chart, and her collectors avidly wait for Sharon's new kits to appear. About 95% of them, she estimates, already know how to do needlework. "I do discourage people who have never threaded a needle from buying my kits, though," Sharon comments, adding, "basically, everyone is capable of doing needlework. If you know the difference between up and down, red and blue, left and right, and an "x" and "o", you can do it."

There are probably three dozen kits in Sharon's line now, with about eight new ones added during an average year. They each contain exactly the same materials Sharon uses for the original, and for her custom work. Silk thread from France is worked on silk gauze in meshes from 40 to 84. The French silks come in a range of about 450 colors, Sharon explains, "mostly European colors which are quite different from American colors.

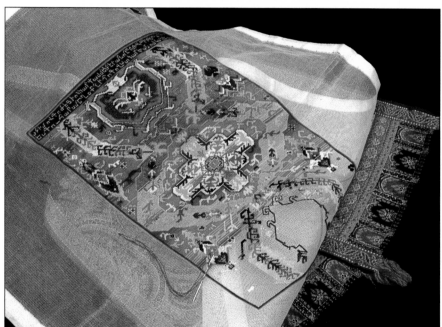

I find that the softer European colors are more appealing for miniatures," she continues, "because along with scaling down the pattern, it's very important to also scale down the colors."

Since she claims to be "uneducated in art," Sharon smiles, "I tend to work with my colors by eye rather than by the book." White might actually be a shade of beige and black a very dark charcoal or navy blue. "If I use orange, it's a very dirty shade of orange," she goes on, "actually

more of a brown tone." Colors change, she has found, depending on what color is next to them.

"The different color variations are very, very important in a Persian carpet," Sharon states, depending on the region where the carpet was made and the dyes that were used for the yarns. "Some of the dyes change color, too," she points out, after years of exposure to light. Sharon takes great pains in both her kits and in her custom work, to accurately re-

produce these nuances of color. It is one of the things that makes her work unique.

When someone buys one of her kits for the first time, Sharon suggests they use one of three stitches to work it: the half cross, the basketweave, or the Continental. "I really like the Continental stitch now," she admits. "It's a challenge to do it well, as it is to do any stitch well. The major factor in which stitch you choose is to use the one you feel you can do best."

Sometimes Sharon's kits come back to her for finishing after the work is completed. She will block them and add fringe if it is called for. "All Persian carpets have fringe," Sharon explains, "but not all needlework carpets are fringed." Often the fringe on full-size antique carpets has an irregular look to it, but Sharon has found that her collectors prefer it to look even and regular on the miniatures. In finishing each carpet, Sharon does not line it because, she says, "the back should be appreciated, too. A lot of times what is underneath is just as exciting, I think, as what you see on the surface."

Sharon signs and dates her work in pen on the margin on the back of each carpet. Pillows are also signed in this way and she often embroiders her initials on the back of each one. "Another form of signature that I use," she confides, "is that any time there is a face, it will have green eyes." Sharon's own eyes are green.

> "I must be doing something with my hands or my mind. If not, I start aggravating the people around me."

It is fortunate for Sharon's personality that her work is as portable as it is. She takes it with her wherever she goes and works at odd moments in a doctor's waiting room or an airport lounge. "I cannot stand sitting still for more than about five minutes without having my work in front of me," she admits. "I must be doing something with my hands or my mind. If not," she laughs, "I start aggravating the people around me."

Sharon finds she spends a great

Sharon's kitchen, seen from the pass-through to the family room, holds a wall full of antique kitchen utensils, mostly in blue. Part of a large spinning wheel can be seen in the center.

deal of time in airports. She travels to shows, lectures or workshops almost one-third of the year. She has lectured at the Cooper-Hewitt Museum in New York, the Museum of the City of New York, and the Allentown, Pennsylvania Art Museum. The shows where she exhibits her work are held all across the country, and she regularly flies to give workshops, a learning experience for herself as well as her students, she feels, "because a lot of times I learn something from my students. I don't know everything," she confesses. "I hope I never do know everything.

"Some people think that I am good; some people think I am the best," Sharon admits, "but I cannot really believe that because then there is no room to grow, and I need that. I need to be challenged, to have my collectors bring me the most impossible project to do." Perhaps it will be that magic carpet in a fairy tale.

Sharon Garmize at work

PHOTO 1 (right): Working from a photograph, a custom order is being stitched directly onto 40 mesh canvas using silk floss.

PHOTO 2 (far right): Various shades of red are being stitched into the background to duplicate the variation in the dye lots which are a common characteristic to full-size Oriental rugs. This is called abrash.

PHOTO 3 (left): A one-of-a-kind Kurdistan carpet is being created. Silk is often threaded out into the margins of the canvas for future use since Sharon really does not know where she is going to stitch next.

PHOTO 4 (above): After the carpets are stitched, charts are then hand drawn for the carpets destined to become kits. The Moresque carpet is shown being charted.

PHOTO 5 (left): Completion of the Moresque chart is supervised by Batchka, Sharon's only ''employee.'' Carpets which are custom orders or one of a kinds are never charted because they are never intended to be repeated.

PHOTO 6 (above): Charting of the Moresque carpet is completed and a new kit is born.

Roger and Nancy Gutheil

Discipline and focused awareness...
contribute to the act of creation.
—*John Poppy*

o you remember what you were doing twenty-five years ago last Wednesday? Most people don't, but Roger Gutheil does. It was the day he responded to a newspaper advertisement that began his career in the crafting of fine miniature furniture.

Before he phoned to answer the advertisement placed by Chestnut Hill Studios, Roger reminisces now, "I thought the ad was to build display models," full-size structures or equipment to be rendered in miniature for an architect, or perhaps, a manufacturer. "Then it turned out to be miniatures," he goes on, "and I thought they were crazy. It just never occurred to me that it would be this kind of miniature."

But the idea was intriguing and Roger decided to give it a try. "I had always worked two jobs," he explains, "and I figured this was a job I could do at home. I wanted to spend

some time at home, see the kids being raised.''

Roger himself was born and raised on Long Island in New York. It was a farming community then, before urbanization crept in, ''and things got crowded,'' he remembers. Roger had thought of becoming a farmer himself, so he enrolled at Cobleskill Community College, upstate, to study agronomy, the theory and practice of field-crop production and soil management. While he was a student there, he met the young, home economics major who would become his wife.

Nancy Yarker had grown up in Greece, New York, a suburb of Rochester, where her parents had apple orchards and a vegetable farm, about 400 acres in all. ''My family goes back to the 1830's in this area,'' Nan comments. ''I've always lived on English Road, except when I lived in the family homestead about three miles over.''

The family farm has been sold off now. Well-cared-for homes occupy the space once devoted to orchards. Roger and Nancy kept a small part of the land and built their Cape Cod-

style home on English Road in 1958. There are half a dozen apple trees and space for a substantial garden in the back yard.

''We could go out and buy the apples a lot cheaper,'' Nan laughs, ''with the cost of spray and the care, but he enjoys doing it.'' Roger also likes to grow vegetables. ''Flowers have never been my thing,'' he admits. ''I'd rather grow vegetables. I love fresh, sweet corn, right off the stalk.'' Much of the produce Roger grows still goes into the two big freezers in the Gutheils' kitchen. ''We had four kids,'' Nan explains, ''so, of course, I used to freeze everything.''

The four Gutheil children — Barbara, Roger, Jr., Richard, and Glenn — were between the ages of three and eleven when their father responded to the newspaper advertisement. Barbara had a dollhouse as a child, but none of the furniture was made by her father. ''I used to make toys for the children,'' Roger recalls, ''rocking horses and things like that, but never anything down into miniature size.''

Roger's basement workshop al-

The dryer/warmer in the bedroom shown at the top of this page is an 18th century piece from Scotland. Roger and Nan love to tour historic houses looking for new designs to add to the collection and found the full-size original of this piece during a European trip. They were allowed to photograph and measure it. The tier table on the left in the photo above was one of Roger's early designs, developed twenty years ago. At the time, it represented the best in miniature furniture available to collectors. Now, that table has evolved into the delicate version on the right.

ready contained many of the full-size tools he uses today. The challenges and possibilities of machinery had always fascinated him. Engineering, he observes, was "something I've always fooled around with." Over the years, Roger has taught himself to use or to repair almost every type of machinery he has been exposed to. "I'll try anything three times before I stop," he insists, "whether it's repairing a furnace, plumbing, whatever. I've always been that way."

Of his working life, Roger claims, "I've been a jack-of-all-trades. I've delivered mail, worked on a golf course on Long Island, installed furnaces, was a weight measurer at a truck scale, did milk testing on cows, worked here on the farm after we were married, and I've been in the hardware business."

> "I'll try anything three times before I stop."

Until miniatures came into his life, it was the hardware business that Roger enjoyed the most, and had spent the most time in. He had been in partnership with his parents in a hardware business in the Hudson Valley before the family moved back to the Rochester area and Roger joined White Wire Works, a specialty metals business where he worked for seventeen years.

At the time Roger first contacted Chestnut Hill Studios, it was also located in a suburb of Rochester not far from where the Gutheils lived. "When it started out," he says of that relationship, "I thought the whole thing was crazy. But, by the time we finished we were doing about 65% of their catalog."

Roger's willingness to experiment, to "try anything at least three times" as he puts it, led to the development of some of the finest miniatures available during the 1960's and early '70's. "The first piece he ever made was the bed warmer," Nan recalls. "When I first started turning the handles," Roger adds, "I was using an electric drill." The metal part was

then soldered to the wooden handle. "Soldering was no problem for me," he remembers. In addition to his electric drill, "I had a table saw, a small planer, a scroll saw, and some hand tools," Roger comments about the contents of his workshop at the time.

"In the beginning, Rog was doing all of it," Nan remembers. "I gradually worked into it, sanding and staining, things like that." The three boys also became interested in the work. "Barbara never really got into it at all," she continues. "The boys did because they were down in the basement with their father." Each had taken a woodworking course at school as he reached the appropriate age, and Roger explains, "I've tried to bring the children up to work with their hands."

Until they went off to college and their own careers, the boys helped with the now-thriving miniatures business. Only Glenn still creates miniature furniture today. Since he is interested in music, he has developed a music stand, the harpsichord, and a spinet pianoforte based on the original at The Essex Institute in Salem, Massachusetts. Roger, Jr., silkscreens the coverlets for the beds.

The Gutheils' part-time involvement in the miniatures business continued until the summer of 1977. By then Chestnut Hill Studios had moved away from Rochester and it became difficult logistically to continue a working relationship. "And I was getting sick and tired of the rush hour traffic," Roger explains, "going up to the city" to his job at White Wire Works. The children were almost off on their own. "We still had one in college," he remembers, "and I decided Nan and I were going to take it easy, go out and hike, do some camping, have some fun," he chuckles now at the recollection. "Instead, it's been 75 or 80 hours a week, seven days a week," Nan adds, in the ten years since they formed Roger L. Gutheil, Incorporated. (Gutheil is pronounced "goot-hile" and means "good health" in German). "It's a real big corporation," Nan laughs, "with two shares of stock. Roger has one and I have the other."

They decided to concentrate on

Roger and Nancy Gutheil (above) are the major, and only, stockholders of Roger L. Gutheil, Incorporated, dedicated to creating the "heirlooms of tomorrow," which they display in "shadow boxes," as they call this handsome library (opposite page, top) with warm, wood paneling and rock maple plank flooring. Furnishings in this room include the C.1790 harpsichord, two tall candlestands, a Queen Anne stool, and a cherry music stand with mahogany finish. A Queen Anne tea table is shown next to the lolling chair, also referred to as a "Martha Washington" chair, with petitpoint upholstery by Stubby Crowe. In the room shown opposite, below, the bonnet top highboy, like many Gutheil pieces, is constructed of cherry with a mahogany finish. The primitive portrait in this room is by Margaret Nines.

producing eighteenth and nineteenth century furniture for the new line, adapting perhaps half a dozen of the pieces they had made before. "They were our favorites," Roger explains. "We had put a lot of work into developing them." Other pieces also were developed and added to the line before the first, signed Gutheil creations were exhibited at a miniature show in late 1977.

During the summer and fall of 1977, "all of the boys pitched in," Roger reminisces. "We designed new pieces. They had the catalog done in about four months' time. It was quite a family effort." Roger, Jr., and a friend of his volunteered to take the line to miniatures shows. "They used to enjoy it," Roger continues. "We still get comments about them," and about the way these two young men presented themselves and the Gutheil line.

They always wore a coat and tie, often three-piece suits, at a time when some miniatures artisans were much more casually dressed. The formality of presentation continues today. During a show, Roger laughs, "I

still cannot take my tie off, even when it's warm in the showroom."

From its inception, the Gutheil line of miniature furniture was presented in a series of lighted display rooms, or shadow boxes as Roger refers to them. "We've had them from the beginning," he explains. "At first they were quite plain, painted walls, fireplace, windows and doors, and that was all. Then we got the time to do a couple of better ones," with paneled walls and more detailed millwork.

The shadow boxes are uniform in their exterior dimensions, with a unique shell construction that allows the interior section to be removed so that the room can more easily be decorated. Roger and Nan have made a few of these room boxes to sell, "mostly as a convenience for our collector customers," Roger notes. "I enjoy making them," he continues. "It's something different."

Room construction usually takes place on the breezeway connecting their house to the garage during the summer months "because of all the sanding," Nan says practically. "The

Although it is not a copy of a specific piece, the handsome slant top desk and bookcase (above right) with its classic, simple crown is typical of the C.1740 period. Working out the construction of the bonnet top secretary (above left) was one of the most difficult things he has ever done, Roger acknowledges. The C.1740 corner cupboard in the room setting shown at the top of the opposite page is the only piece in the Gutheil collection that is available unfinished because some collectors prefer to paint a corner cupboard the same color as the walls or woodwork. The four poster bed (opposite, below) is topped by a tester rail and features typical Early American bed hangings of crewel embroidery by Frances Exley. Next to it is a unique chest-on-chest-on-chest, made in three separate parts. It has brass bale handles on the ends of each section.

dust blows out and it keeps the house cleaner."

No matter what season of the year, the work day begins early in the Gutheil household. Nan is a "morning person, very definitely," she states. "I can work all night," Roger admits, "but I hate to get up in the morning.

She's up at five o'clock, gets me up at six, and by seven o'clock we're both down in the basement.''

Almost the whole basement has been taken over for the production of miniatures. "This used to be a playroom for the kids," Roger says about his workshop. "Almost all the tools I have down here are on wheels," so they can be moved around as each one is needed. "This is where it all starts," he continues, pointing out the planer at the end of the workshop. "We buy the lumber, mostly cherry and maple, an inch and a quarter rough. I plane my own wood because that way I can control the thicknesses." The planer, he says, "makes an awful noise." Nan adds, with a grimace, that "it sounds like someone scratching a blackboard," even from her workbench at the far side of the large basement.

Nan's part of the process involves mostly handwork; sanding and finishing is her specialty. It is something she has become extremely adept at. "Nan can close her eyes, run her fingers over a piece of wood, and tell you which way the grain is going," Roger marvels. "I don't have the touch you have," he says to her. Patience is what it takes, Nan believes. "It's just a matter of having the sandpaper and using it," and a magnifying glass. "Yes, I use one," she admits. "You examine the piece at an angle,

turn it and look at it again, to make sure you get all the sander marks off. Otherwise,'' she feels, ''the stain won't penetrate as well.

"We've just learned over the years," Nan continues. "We're still learning," Roger adds. "We still make mistakes."

Roger seldom loses his temper over a piece he is working on, but admits that the bonnet top secretary caused him to do just that when it was still in the design stage. "The only piece I ever threw against the cellar wall was the bonnet top when I first made it," he laughs. "I used to think about how to make that top, get out the sketch paper and figure out how I was going to make the cutters, how to do the bows and have them match. Finally, I thought I had it solved," he continues, "and I started working on it, but it just wouldn't match."

Pieces of that particular puzzle were on the basement floor when ''Nan tried to calm me down,'' Roger goes on. ''She picked them up, arranged them, and said, how does this look. It was just the reverse of the way I was doing it. All of a sudden things just fell into place, but oh, the frustration.''

Over the years both Roger and Nan have developed their own special ways of doing things, and they are always willing to share their hints with other craftsmen, but not, they say,

Two examples of pieces built during Roger and Nan's early years of creating miniatures are shown on this page. The bed warmer (above) is the very first miniature Roger made. He turned the wooden handle with an electric drill. The fireplace on the left (top) is an early piece, while the other, with Delft tiles by Marie Friedman, is from their current collection. The quilt on the bed pictured opposite is by the Gutheils' eldest son, Roger Gutheil, Jr., who silkscreens quilts for several beds in the collection.

through teaching classes. Since Roger was named a Fellow in the International Guild of Miniatures Artisans in 1980, he has been asked to teach at the I.G.M.A. school, and has declined. "That's not my forte," he feels. "Doing it is one thing, but trying to teach someone else to do it another. Besides," he confesses, "I get up in front of any more than six people and I'll start stuttering and get very nervous."

What they both do enjoy is meeting and talking with their collectors at shows. When they can see people discover and appreciate the work they do, "the satisfaction we get is really something," Roger confides. Before or after a show, Roger and Nan will often find time to stop at a museum or an historic house. "We love to look at furniture," Nan admits of these "busman's holidays." They have been to Williamsburg and Winterthur as well as to many lesser-known places, searching for and studying fine furniture. Most of the pieces they choose for the line are adapted from their antique counterparts, but Roger and Nan also produce some exact reproductions of furniture from the Margaret Woodbury Strong Museum in Rochester.

> "When it started out, I thought the whole thing was crazy."

One of the curators at the Museum "approached us," Roger recalls, when the Museum was still in the planning stages, "and wanted to know if we'd be interested in making miniatures of the full-size American Empire furniture in the collection." They were taken on a tour, and allowed to choose the pieces they thought could successfully be reproduced in miniature. The American Empire period is not as popular or as well-known as some other periods of furniture design, but these Gutheil miniatures represent some of the best work done in the pillar and scroll style in America during the mid-1800's.

The six examples of American Em-

pire furniture Roger developed were all added to the Gutheil line during a fairly short span of time. "Ideally," he says, "we should add four or six new pieces every year. It would be good for our collectors, and good for us because it's a different pace, the challenge of making something new." The problem, or the "buggerboo" as Roger puts it, is the time factor. They find themselves working against a stack of orders for the pieces they already produce. "I hate to make people wait," Roger admits. The number of hours in their day stays the same; the number of hours it takes to create each piece does not change. "It's reaching the point where we have to ease off," Nan says reluctantly. "We don't want to stop," she insists, "but we have to ease off from the number of hours we work each week."

On the other hand, their success in creating the "heirlooms of tomorrow" has brought them both a full measure of satisfaction. It is something neither Roger nor Nancy Gutheil had any idea might happen those twenty-five years ago last Wednesday.

Roger and Nancy Gutheil at work

PHOTO 1: Roger is surface planing 1-1/2'' rough cherry lumber on the thickness planer.

PHOTO 2: He resaws the plank to 1/8th'' on a band saw.

PHOTO 3 (above): On a table saw, he rips cherry wood to the correct width.

PHOTO 4 (right): Still using the table saw, Roger cuts cherry wood pieces to length.

PHOTO 5 (right): The table saw with a cross cutting jig on it.

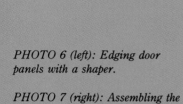

PHOTO 6 (left): Edging door panels with a shaper.

PHOTO 7 (right): Assembling the base for a library shelf.

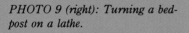

PHOTO 8 (left): Assembling the door panel for a library shelf.

PHOTO 9 (right): Turning a bedpost on a lathe.

PHOTO 10 (left): Sanding the base of the library shelf with a belt sander.

PHOTO 11 (right): Nan checks a piece for excess glue.

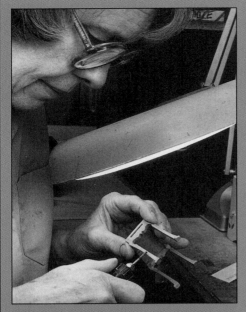

PHOTO 12 (left): Nan is roughing out tea table legs prior to the final carving.

PHOTO 13 (right): She is rubbing the tea table base with steel wool.

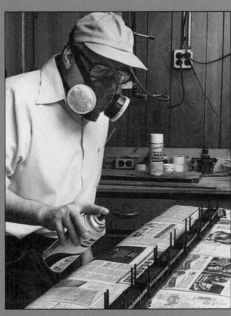

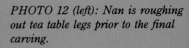

PHOTO 14 (left): Applying stain to a Queen Anne sideboard.

PHOTO 15 (right): Spraying finish on several completed Queen Anne sideboards.

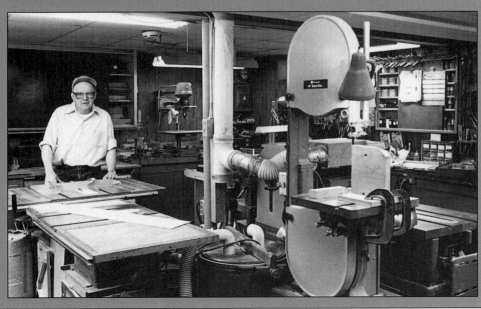

PHOTO 16 (left): A partial view of the shop, showing the full-size tools used to make Gutheil miniatures.

Cabinet by Roger and Nancy Gutheil; silver by Peter Acquisto; birds by Mary McGrath.

Renee Bowen was born in Cleveland, Ohio, went to school in the Midwest, and majored in Spanish in college. "I have no art background at all," Renee confesses. "I've always been interested in working with my hands, always very comfortable with needle and thread and I've done a lot of sewing, a lot of needlework, almost every form there is," she believes.

> "I had been meeting people who were interested in miniatures...I was captivated by them."

Moving to Boston, and noting that "one thing leads to another," Renee explains that a new friend talked her into having her ears pierced. "That was like the turning point in my life, a really stupid thing," she comments now. But, since she "couldn't afford to buy earrings, I started making them. Well, within minutes, I had an earring business going. I was making and selling earrings all over the country," at the rate of some two thousand pairs of earrings a month. This was during the 1960's, during the "Hippie" culture influenced by Haight-Ashbury. Renee's product was very popular, especially with young people.

"Then I met a fellow who had an antiques shop that he just couldn't afford to keep open," Renee recalls. He couldn't afford to hire her, but suggested that she could keep the shop open, selling his stock for him as well as her earrings for her own profit. It was a workable arrangement until "he decided just overnight that he was going to move," and left Renee with both her own business which was doing very well, and the antiques, "which I knew very little about, so I just got out the books and started studying," she says simply.

"He left, I took over his shop, and just started learning about antiques until I gradually filled up the shop," Renee continues. The shop was located in an area of Boston where there were "Lots of old-time antiques dealers," Renee explains,

"who took me under their wing and taught me about the business. They were all very gracious, very nice about it."

Renee kept the earring business, added antique accessories, and then "old fashioned clothing when that was really popular in the '60's. I was getting attics full of the stuff, delivered by truck, and the young people were buying it up. Oh, it was fabulous," she enthuses. "We'll never see days like that again," she adds, recalling the lines of people outside, waiting to get into her small shop on a Saturday. "The line was sometimes two blocks long and it would last all day."

Unfortunately, this was also a time of great unrest in many college com-

Jim was fascinated when he saw a photograph of the full-size original of this clock, and drew a sketch of it. "Then I went to the museum where the clock was on exhibit, with this drawing, not to scale. The curator opened up the glass case and we measured the clock," he recalls. "I just filled in the measurements on the drawing. There was no scale to it; I just filled in the blanks." Jim then drew an accurate plan and began making the miniature. "This clock is very difficult to build," he notes, "because everything has to fit. It is just very exacting."

munities, of riots and violence, and Renee's business was by no means immune. She had opened a second shop near Harvard Square in Cambridge,

Renee has reproduced in miniature the curlew decoy pictured in the window at right. The full-size, flame birch-topped table in this photo was made by Jim. The corner cupboard in the dining room (above) is the last full-size piece he built before the miniatures took over.

operated it successfully for two years, and then "the riots broke out and I was tear-gassed," she remembers. She was outside her shop there when "I saw this mob of people coming in my direction, so I turned and ran back into my shop and locked the door, just in time to look out the window and see police, tear gas, billy clubs, the whole nine yards!"

Renee was trapped for the duration in her shop which was filling up with tear gas, "trying to hide out in the back of the building until the worst of it was over," she explains. When the incident was repeated a week later, "that's when the decision was made to move to Maine," Renee states matter-of-factly.

She settled in the Kennebunk area, joining two friends in an antiques business for a time, before she bought a house, and "moved my part of the business into my own house, living above the shop. And that's

where I started making miniatures," she explains. "I had been meeting people who were interested in miniatures. I had never even noticed them before that, but I was captivated by them."

Renee decided she would like to reproduce antique furniture in miniature, the kind "I knew I would never be able to find, to be able to own," she notes, "nice, quality, wonderful antiques. I started out with a few Shaker things because the lines were simple. I thought they would be a little easier to make."

Renee recalls being aware of one-twelfth scale, but not of having any books or diagrams to follow. "I was just getting antiques, measuring

them, and copying them," she continues. "After I moved to Alfred to be with Jim, I thought it would be great if I really started to get into this. All the pieces he was doing in full-scale, I would do in miniature," she decided, "because he had measured them all, right? Save me all that work," she smiles.

This arrangement continued in Paris Hill, until Jim built that first Shaker desk in miniature, the salesman's sample. Then, "no more big furniture," Renee comments. "That did it." Renee still builds furniture in the Shaker style because "I love it," but Jim seldom does now. "He wanted to move on," she explains, and has explored many other styles, although specializing in American country decorated furniture built from about 1700 to the late 1800's. Even though the Shaker style continues to appear in their collection from time to time, both Jim and Renee prefer not to be categorized. ''People tend to do this to both of us,'' Renee notes, wondering if that means ''they think this is the only thing you can make. Jim's work has certainly evolved into many different areas, and I hope that mine has, too.''

Jim is especially interested at the moment in country decorated pieces that originated in New England. ''Every now and then,'' he explains, ''I see a piece of decorated furniture that just happens to be Pennsylvania, and if I like it, I will make it. But since we live in Maine, New England is more where our feelings lie.

''There's something about the New England pieces,'' he believes. ''They are more one-of-a-kind, each one is so different. Often, they were made by a person who made, maybe only one piece in his whole lifetime, and decorated. Who knows why he decorated it the way he did,'' Jim muses. ''It's absolutely fascinating to me, some of those pieces. You look at them and wonder why he or she made a particular design, what is it supposed to represent. It's really neat.''

> ''You are more
> patient with your
> miniatures. It can
> go wrong and you
> will correct it
> because you won't
> settle for anything
> less.''

Jim's interest in decorated pieces came about over a period of time. At first, it was ''mostly just painting one color pieces,'' he recalls. ''Now it's hard for me to think about doing a piece that is not decorated in some way,'' or antiqued with some signs of wear. Doing something to the surface of the piece is, for Jim, a way of creating its history.

''What's happening in this piece,''

he explains, holding a paneled chest he has been working on, to illustrate, ''is that it was probably painted red at one time, and then they painted it white to cover the red. Then they painted it green and decorated it. What you are seeing is that some of the green has worn off and the white is coming through; in places, the red is coming through,'' he points out.

In order to achieve this look, Jim continues, ''first, I'll do a red coat, paint the whole thing red, and then just rub it down, sand it a little bit because it may have been red for years and there would be some wear. Then,'' he adds, ''they would have painted the whole thing white because they wanted to paint the panels, so I do that next, paint the whole thing white and frame it with the green. Now it starts to really have some nice depth,'' he believes.

''I will sometimes put on three or four different coats of paint just to give it that sort of depth, so there is something about it that causes you to wonder what's going on there, where is that color coming from. That is time-consuming,'' Jim admits, but worth it, ''because you are trying to do the same thing to the piece that was done to the original. The only way you can do it is to follow the same sort of life that piece had.''

Sometimes Jim keeps a written guide to show what steps in painting

Renee designed this adaption of an old peddler doll with a cupboard bottom, ''a happy looking peddler,'' she points out. ''Peddler dolls were always very sour-looking, which I didn't like.'' The dolls have jointed arms and are available unfinished like the one in the center, or dressed. Renee says she prefers to allow her customers to decorate and fill the cupboard bottom, and notes that they are adaptable to many themes.

each piece were taken, and he usually keeps written step-by-step building instructions and measurements, especially of his more complicated pieces of furniture, such as a tall case clock currently in the collection.

Renee, on the other hand, keeps very few notes. ''I try to save at least one piece,'' she admits, ''because I'm lost without it. If I have the piece in front of me, I can intuitively see what I have to do first, second and third. Without it,'' she confesses, ''I think, oh, dear, I don't even know where to start.''

''She never takes any of my advice,'' Jim chides, gently. ''In fact, what I do every so often, is make another set of notes, just to see how I've changed the styles, techniques or process.''

Even though Renee makes a conscious effort to save at least one example of everything she makes, and Jim does not, they both have a difficult time keeping their shop showcases

Renee's rug designs (right) are reproduced from old New England patterns, some exact even to the overall measurements and some adapted to be more appropriate to miniature work and to the medium used. The table (above) is filled with the rug kits she has designed. In the background is the silk-screen, framed, that was used to print the pattern on the fabric. A Nutshell News Product Review said, ''The kit is easy to work and takes less concentration than other forms of miniature needlework. There is no counting...just filling in a printed area with French knots.''

filled, or to have enough stock on hand to be able to exhibit and sell at many shows.

''When people come into the shop,'' Jim explains, ''I feel they really deserve special treatment. They have made the effort to come up and see us here, and I really like to cater to them.'' Often, these are collectors who come back year after year, who are knowledgeable antiques collectors in many cases, and ''who have never collected a miniature in their lives,'' Jim insists. ''They just liked something they saw in here, and decided they would really like to have it. And I suppose,'' he continues, ''I would hope, that another reason is that something happens when you go into someone's shop, something special. It's their environment, their workshop, and you see them working....'' Renee adds, ''You have a rapport.''

Jim believes, ''It's very exciting, and something we really try to en-

''I did a couple of Shaker pieces...I was drawn to that part of their culture, really intrigued with their furniture.''

courage, to cultivate,'' not considering it an interruption of their working time. ''It's never been a problem. It's always nice when people come in,'' he says. ''I try to plan around the possibility of that happening throughout the day, and usually try to wait until evening to start painting anything that I'm going to be really involved in.''

Renee credits Jim's relaxed attitude with the fact that he can ''cope better than I can,'' she says. Also ''you are more patient with your miniatures,'' she tells him. ''It can go wrong and you will correct it because you won't settle for anything less. Oh, you may agonize over it for awhile, but not out loud. I remember when you were making big furniture,'' she confides, ''and if something went wrong, the whole town knew it.''

> *''There was something about the New England pieces. They are more one-of-a-kind, each one is so different.''*

Jim believes that ''has to do with the fact that all your effort is concentrated on the piece you are making. I enjoy that,'' he adds, recalling the frustrations of trips to the hardware store and to Massachusetts to buy lumber for his full-sized furniture. ''I didn't enjoy all the preparation involved in what I had to go through with the full-sized pieces,'' he admits.

These days, their trips are often forays to museums to research and measure the antiques they make in miniature. Since they prefer Maine-made pieces, one of their favorite research sites is the Maine State Museum. It was on a visit there that they discovered the perfect name for their business.

''We needed a name for our shop because we were moving from Paris Hill and couldn't take that name with us,'' Jim explains, ''and we saw an exhibit of tin at the Maine State Museum.'' Tin has been a material traditionally used for gifts commemorating a tenth wedding anniversary. One of the items in the exhibit was a feather, ''a tinsmith's whimsy,'' he adds, ''quite large. And we had really spent months trying to figure out what to call ourselves, and kept going back to The Tin Feather. We wanted something that was a little bit catchy, and it worked,'' he concludes.

It is also a name the pair can take with them, ''because we are somewhat nomadic,'' Renee admits. For the time being, though, they are well-settled in Kennebunk. Jim has recently served as Chairman of the annual Winter Carnival. Renee insists that she ''just likes the feeling of the community, of living in it.'' Although their shop is quite different from some of the other businesses in the town, ''it has been very interesting,'' Jim believes, ''getting to meet these people, small business people like we are, and seeing how they try to solve

Although their work is based on careful research, Jim and Renee have also developed their own working techniques through experimentation. ''I don't know too much about the technical part of painting,'' Jim comments about this beautifully decorated domed-top box (above left), ''and every now and then I think about taking a workshop. Then I decide that I'm doing OK, just as I'm doing now. I think I like that.'' Renee also has her own self-taught system of making reproduction Shaker furniture (above). ''Of all the different things I make, these are the only notes I have,'' she confesses, holding three or four small scraps of paper, an impish grin on her face. When she is reproducing a piece she has already made before, she much prefers to look at the piece as she works. ''If I have the piece in front of me, I can intuitively see what I have to do first, second and third,'' she feels. All of the pieces in this group are Shaker-inspired; the yellow dry sink is copied from one exactly like it at Sabbathday Lake, Maine, a still-viable Shaker community where Jim and Renee made friends with the Shakers and were able to measure and copy their furniture.

problems and help one another.''

Even though their business is ''really outside the realm of normal, business-type establishments,'' as Jim puts it, it is hard to imagine this creative pair of artisans in any endeavor other than the one that initially started with one special, salesman's sample.

Jim Hastrich at work

PHOTO 1 (above): Jim turns the leg for a tavern table on a lathe. PHOTO 2 (right): The leg is mortised out with a small drill press. PHOTO 3 (below left): Jim cuts a tenon to fit the mortised leg. PHOTO 4 (below right): The tenon is fitted into the mortise.

PHOTO 5 & 6 (above and right): Jim drills holes into the top of the leg to hold the skirt of the table in place.

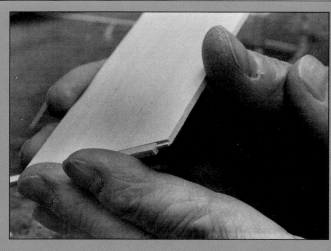

PHOTO 7: Jim is rabbeting (making a groove) for the "bread board end" of the table top.

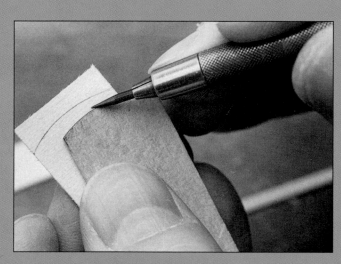

PHOTO 8: The grooved piece is fitted onto the tongue at the end of the table top piece.

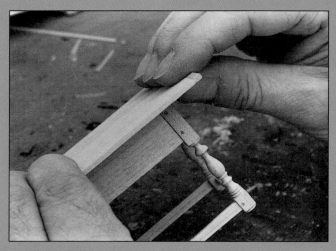

PHOTO 9: The table top is glued onto the bottom of the table, and it is complete.

PHOTO 10: Now Jim is preparing to make a dome-top box. He is using a template to draw the correct curve onto the sides of the box.

PHOTO 11: After drawing the curve, he cuts away all the extra wood, so that all that remains is the end of the box.

PHOTO 12: The sides, ends and bottom of the box have been assembled.

PHOTO 13: *After steaming and molding the top piece around a dowel, Jim glues it onto the box.*

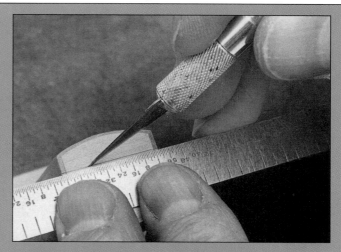

PHOTO 14: *He cuts around the box so that it can open.*

PHOTO 15: *A hinge is fabricated from wire; the tails of the hinge are trimmed off after it is attached to box.*

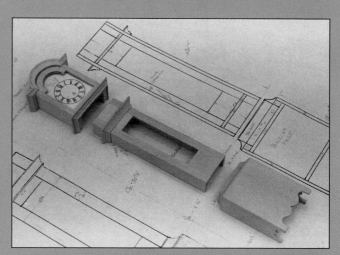

PHOTO 16: *A partially finished clock, in three sections, is shown with Jim's measured drawings for building it.*

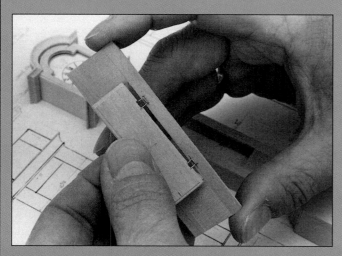

PHOTO 17: *A door is attached to the center section, using hinges made similarly to those in Photo 15.*

PHOTO 18: *The bonnet of the clock with the dial, frame piece and door, in the process of assembly.*

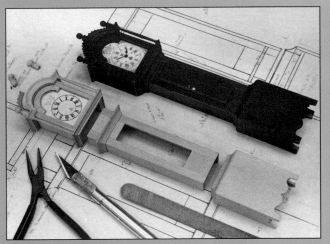

PHOTO 19: A completed clock is pictured along with one that is still in three sections, Jim's basic tools, and measured drawings.

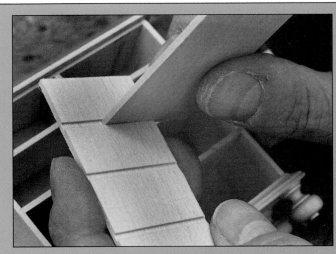

PHOTO 20: The sides of a five-drawer chest that Jim is making have been dadoed to accept the shelves.

PHOTO 21: After the shelves are in place, Jim carefully applies the molding around the bottom of the chest.

*Renee Bowen carves
a curlew decoy*

PHOTO 1: Renee traces the curlew pattern onto a small block of wood.

PHOTO 2: She roughs out around the tracing with a small saw.

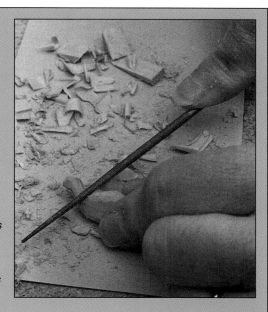

PHOTO 3 (left): Rounded edges and detailing are done with an X-acto knife.

PHOTO 4 (right): Renee shapes the curves with a round file.

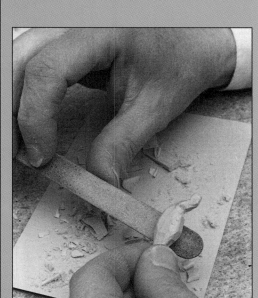

PHOTO 5 (left): Sanding is done with an emery board.

PHOTO 6 (right): She notches the tail with a file.

PHOTO 7 (left): The evolution of the curlew decoy is shown here, including some of the tools Renee uses in making it.

Marjorie Meyer

. . .Blossom by blossom the spring begins.
—Algernon Charles Swinburne

HELP WANTED. Position entails crafting miniature objects. Unique combination of skills necessary. Successful applicant will have a lively imagination, should be perfectionist with highly developed sense of humor, and willing to work 10-12 hours per day. Full-time, year-round occupation. Experience required. Fringe benefits.

*I*f you could design the perfect job description for her, the one above would fit Marjorie Meyer to a "T". Growing up in Cincinnati, Ohio, where

she still lives, Marjorie always had a strong make-believe trait in her genes.

It was on a Christmas Eve when she was about ten years old, that Marjorie crouched near the decorated tree, her knees drawn up to her chin, alone with her dreams of what the packages with her name on them might contain. Tentatively, she touched one, feeling its shape, imagining what must be inside. A set of paints, she decided, pretty colors of paints in containers, with brushes and paper.

"I always wanted to be an artist," Marjorie insists, "and when I felt that

one and thought, this is a set of paints, I was so excited.'' When she opened the mysterious package the next morning and found it was a school bag instead, ''I still remember the horrible disappointment I felt,'' she laughs, recalling the story today.

Marjorie's only sibling, a brother four years older, had friends of his own and wasn't much interested in spending time with his younger sister. ''I wanted so much for them to pay attention to me,'' Marjorie recalls, ''so of course, I was always

Marjorie and Stan Meyer, married 40 years, relax in the comfortable family room of their home (top). She is weaving a piece of miniature wicker which will eventually be a chair. At above right, full-size honeysuckle forms a fragrant background for Marjorie's miniature greenhouse, built by Stan from a kit for Marjorie to fill with her own plants and flowers. The brick path is made of papier mache egg cartons. At right is one of four sets of tiny houses Marjorie made for each of her children. The first house the family lived in is on the right. In the back is the second, ''my contemporary period,'' Marjorie notes. On the left is the house they owned before moving into their new townhouse.

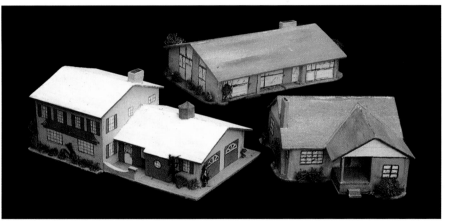

On the far left is the bed in the miniature room Marjorie created as part of the Miniature Society of Cincinnati's "Retirement Village" several years ago. On the right is the full-size bed in Marjorie and Stan's bedroom — a reversal of the usual process of miniaturizing full-size items. She hadn't realized when she designed the full-size treatment recently that she had already created one in miniature. The painting in the background of the photo below, left, is one of Marjorie's favorites from the art classes she took some years ago. "There's a certain uniqueness to it," she believes, "and I never tire of it."

underfoot.'' There was even a time, she claims, ''when they tied me to a tree and threw apples at me. My brother thought I was a brat. I thought he was wonderful, but mean,'' she laughs. One of her brother's friends at that time was Stan Meyer.

When World War II started, both Stan and Marjorie's brother went into the Army. Only Stan came home. Her brother ''died in 1943 in a plane crash in the Army,'' she says quietly. ''I guess the best part is that he's still 20. I've seen some of his friends and they've grown older, but he's still that Adonis. There is some consolation in that,'' she observes, ''but I feel cheated. I think we would have been close.''

> *"I thought scale was a skin condition, or the outside of a fish."*

During the war years when they were home on leave, her brother's friends always came to visit Marjorie's mother. ''My mother was greatly loved by all these young men,'' she remembers. In 1944 Stan came to visit when he was home on leave. ''This time I managed to get his attention,'' Marjorie remembers. ''He took me out for a drive and that was the beginning. Forty years later, here we are,'' she smiles, adding, ''I guess we did something right.''

For the rest of the time Stan was away, Marjorie faithfully wrote letters

to him and worked at the job she had had since high school, selling cosmetics. ''I was rather proud of the fact that at eighteen, I was managing the shop,'' she remarks. ''I made $45 a week and that was a fortune.''

Stan had started college on the G.I. Bill when he and Marjorie married and began their family. ''The children came fast and furiously,'' she recalls of those busy, early years. ''It was very difficult for Stan to study, be a father and a husband,'' all at the same time, ''and money was hard to come by,'' she remembers.

The Meyers have four children. Their son lives in Texas, but their three daughters are in Ohio. ''I have two married daughters living here in Cincinnati. We are the best of friends,'' she comments happily.

''My husband and my sons-in-law are thoroughly convinced,'' Marjorie confides, ''that my daughters and I have a language of our own. We can talk, begin a sentence, and the other one finishes it. We know what we are talking about, but the men just sit there with their mouths open, not believing it. There's a great stream running through all of us,'' she continues, ''the cause of much laughter and many tears.''

One Christmas Marjorie had made tiny cardboard models of the three houses the family had lived in during the children's growing up years. They were miniature in size, but not in any particular scale. ''At that time,'' Marjorie remarks, ''I thought scale was a skin condition, or the outside of a fish.'' She gave a set of the houses to each child, ''and we all cried buckets of tears,'' she reminisces, ''thinking of all the things that had happened in each of the houses. They loved it. I am so blessed to have such loving children.''

During their growing up years, Marjorie spent most of her time with the children. ''I never had babysitters,'' she remembers. Later, when they were in school and she had free time, ''I would rather stay home and work on a project,'' she explains. ''I have always loved doing things with my hands.'' She sewed clothes for the three girls, and ''for years I made all of our Christmas cards. That was hard to stop,'' she notes, ''because people expect it year after year. But it was fun.''

> ''Someone described me as a low-brow high-brow, and I think that's accurate.''

Marjorie worked part-time during those years in the animation studio of a film company which produced televi-

The art of egg decorating, as inspired by Faberge, has captivated many artists who are attracted to fine detail and elegance. Before miniatures came into her life, Marjorie created 1,500 eggs such as these in sizes up to the ostrich egg (above left). Many of the backgrounds in the eggs are copied from rooms in historic homes.

sion commercials. ''I didn't drive at the time,'' Marjorie recalls, ''but they thought enough of me to come and pick me up every day, and bring me back home.'' Two artists did the original drawings, she continues, ''and I would do their follow-up work, putting them on a cell. It taught me to appreciate how much goes into each second of an animated bit of work. It's very difficult,'' she found, ''to take the very flat paint used on those cells and make a food look appetizing, make it look three-dimensional.''

After this job, Marjorie decided to take an art course, taught by a nun at a local high school. ''I enjoyed it thoroughly,'' she remembers. ''Sister Elizabeth really taught me to observe, to see the colors in a tree, to see how a tree is made. God does a good job,'' she had concluded. Before the course was finished, her teacher told Marjorie that she ''ought to have a one-man show,'' Marjorie recalls. ''and I nearly fell over from flattery. Wasn't that a lovely, sweet thing for her to say? We had a great rapport.''

Although she never had that one-

Marjorie has made only one 1/4-inch scale setting (top). "That was more or less done as a joke to myself, I guess," she admits, "but I like it." Pictured above are examples of her most prolific work: plants and wicker, set off by a stained glass-like framed window. On the opposite page, is a gourd that Marjorie has made into a home for Fern, "a woodland fairy and the daughter of a nymph and an unknown gnome."

workroom. "I can't tell you how soothing that is to me" she says of this work which looks as though it might be a quilted fabric hanging. "I've never tired of it. There is just something peaceful about it, cozy, an orderly layout." Admitting that she is basically an orderly, neat person, Marjorie confides, "I can't believe what a mess I can make of my workroom. But I love neatness. I only wish someone else would create the neatness for me. That would be fun."

> *"My husband and my sons-in-law are thoroughly convinced that my daughters and I have a language of our own."*

Until about ten years ago, Marjorie used her work space to create decorated eggs. Although there are only about 30 still in her possession, and on display in their home, Marjorie estimates that she has created about 1,500 of them. Most were sold and given away as gifts over the years.

"I was always searching for the little things to put into them," Marjorie remembers, at craft or gift shops until one day she stopped at a miniatures shop. Until then, she admits, "I didn't know a thing about miniatures, but that did it!" Now, she claims, "I would rather shop for miniature furniture than I would for real-size furniture. It gives me such satisfaction."

Marjorie immediately set about creating her first box room as a surprise birthday present for Stan. "I know it was the greatest gift I've ever given him," she says of the miniature post office incorporating his stamp collecting hobby, as well as some of his other favorite things.

Next came a Christmas room and Marjorie began crafting miniatures of some of the ornaments from their full-size tree. She became a "hobbyist gone crazy," she confesses, as miniatures began taking over her creative imagination. She and Stan joined the Miniature Society of Cincinnati, an active and talented group; some of its

man show, several of Marjorie's paintings hang in the Meyers' home in a suburb of Cincinnati. "This is one of the paintings Sister really loved," Marjorie points out during a tour of her home. "She handed me a Christmas card and told me to copy it. I love how it turned out," she continues.

Another painting from that period hangs over the desk in Marjorie's members have become her closest friends. ''It's marvelous,'' she feels, ''I treasure them, I really do.''

Marjorie's next few years were spent learning and experimenting with miniatures in many mediums. She made a tiny ''electric'' blanket because ''I wanted to do something that no one else had done,'' she remembers, and called it ''an energy-saver, because it didn't really work.'' She made fruits and vegetables of bread dough, wicker-look furniture, leather-covered trunks, wooden rocking horses, ''stained glass'' windows, tennis racquets ''strung'' with a scrap of one daughter's wedding veil fabric, and the list goes on. ''You can wander far afield with miniatures,'' Marjorie truly believes, ''and that's lovely.''

About half a dozen years ago Marjorie zeroed in on the two types of miniatures she enjoys making the most, paper flowers and her special wicker furniture. ''I love flowers. I love doing them,'' she admits. ''That's really peaceful to me. I don't know what else I want to get into now, except for trying other flowers, and continuing with the wicker.''

> ''You can wander far afield with miniatures, and that's lovely.''

Marjorie still has the first piece of wicker furniture she made, out of a pink straw hat. ''It's not great,'' she insists, ''but it was the inspiration for what came after it. But, I knew if I wanted to do more, I'd either have to buy an awful lot of hats, or find some other method of making them.'' She decided to try needlepoint canvas.

''I am most proud of the one I call the 'cozy' design,'' Marjorie continues, ''and the Newport. The 'cozy' design is brown, antiqued, and I copied the first one from a photograph I had seen in a magazine. I loved the antique look of it, but it takes five coats of paint to get the finish I like on that piece of furniture.'' Marjorie's Newport design is white,

''summery-looking,'' she observes. ''Somehow, I think you can feel the breeze blowing through that chair,'' conveying a feeling of fantasy and perfection that is possible in the miniature world.

That feeling of perfection is also present in Marjorie's plants and flower arrangements. The colors never fade, the flowers will not

droop; they remain exactly as she creates them. ''I love the paper,'' she remarks. ''It gives me the thinness that I need.'' After the paper is painted in the colors she wants the flowers and plants to be, Marjorie uses a die to cut some of the petals and leaves, and hand-cuts all the rest.

An assortment of live plants and flowers are usually in her workroom

Marjorie's flower arrangements are always fresh and crisp as a summer breeze. Gladioli, tiger lilies, delphinium, poppies, daisies and roses are just a few of the flowers she combines into colorful arrangements.

because "I love the real thing," Marjorie confides. "Seeing which leaves are glossy, which ones are more of a matte finish, that helps so much. I admit that silk flowers have helped me a lot, too. There are some wonderful artisans," she believes, "who work in silk flowers and I have copied some of those.

"I like to wander in the florist shops," Marjorie continues. "I'm always looking for new ideas, to see what kind of flowers it is possible for me to do. There are some flowers I just can't do; the paper has to bend a certain way." One of the most complicated plants Marjorie makes is the fuchsia. "It could drive me bananas," she laughs, with all its various, tiny parts.

Another difficult arrangement is a hanging geranium with some vinca vine. "Each leaf has to be painted and edged with white," she explains, "and every leaf for the geranium is hand-cut," and perfectly cut, besides, because Marjorie is the kind of person who will only accept perfection. "Probably one of my biggest problems," she admits. "Miss Perfect," is what she claims Stan calls her in his moments of irritation. "I expect perfection," Marjorie con-

fesses, "and that's hard to live with sometimes."

To achieve her own standard of perfection in her miniatures, Marjorie works ten or twelve hours almost every day. "When you can do that and never tire of it," she insists, "that's a good job, isn't it." Her daytime hours are usually spent in her workroom and a friend of hers once complained that "Marjorie is the only person I know who never has time to just go out to lunch."

Once a month Marjorie and Stan get together with nine other couples who belong to a dinner club. "We've been in it twenty years," she relates, "so we've watched each other grow older. Sometimes we do absolutely ridiculous things, and laugh a lot. We are very different people, and yet if anything goes wrong, we help each other."

> *"I love neatness. I only wish someone else would create the neatness for me."*

Some evenings they go to concerts. "Someone described me as a low-brow high-brow," Marjorie confides, "and I think that's accurate," adding that she likes light symphony and pop concerts, "but I'm not into Beethoven and Bach." At home, when she is working, Marjorie "listens to the television, sort of like oldtime radio," she says.

The wide acceptance of her work in miniature has added an important dimension to Marjorie's life. "I'm proud of what I do," she admits. "I have so much more self-confidence now than I used to have. Of course, it's all those lovely pats on the back. It's been good for me. I'm a happier person."

Marjorie Meyer has grown from the shy, little girl who desperately wanted a set of paints and got a school bag instead, to an accomplished miniaturist who "brings fantasy into the real world," as she puts it. That transition must have been been possible because of that strong make-believe trait in her genes.

Marjorie Meyer creates a hanging plant

PHOTO 1: A view of some of Marjorie's tools, a finished hanging geranium, pink geranium, caladium, containers for leaves and blossoms, dogwood and gladiola.

PHOTO 2: Marjorie is cutting leaves from folded paper for a hanging geranium . In the background are a hanging pot, caladium leaves, finished caladium, and wires for hanging the geranium.

PHOTO 3: Still cutting the paper, a finished geranium is shown in the background.

PHOTO 4 (above): She punches out geranium petal forms from painted tracing paper.

PHOTO 5 (left): The petals are placed on the ball which is the foundation for the geranium blossom. Glue is kept ready for use in a bottle cap, a handy container for a small amount of glue or paint.

PHOTO 6: Marjorie has already put wire over the main branch of wire to form branches, and is now putting on the hand-cut leaves. A finished branch and hanging pot are seen in the background.

PHOTO 7: She always adds vinca vine to her hanging geraniums. The leaves for the vine are punched out with a heart-shaped punch, and then each leaf is edged with white paint. The leaves are then placed on a green thread to form a vine.

PHOTO 8: Marjorie is holding the pot by the cord hanger, and is gluing in a finished stem.

PHOTO 9: She is finishing by putting the vinca vine in place. Needed support for the plant is provided by her handy tool, the Third Hand, sometimes called the Helping Hand.

Top photo: Breakfront and slant-top desk by Roger Gutheil; silver by Peter Acquisto; cats by Charles Claudon; flowers by Marjorie Meyer; Hummel figurine "Stormy Weather" by Robert Olszewski. Above: Blanket chest, press cupboard (left in photo), Shaker cupboard (right in photo) and document box by Jim Hastrich; yarn winder, food safe and sifter by Renee Bowen.

Robert Olszewski

Imagination is the beginning of creation.
—George Bernard Shaw

Millions of people have seen his work. Many of them recognize his name instantly, and consider him an artist without peer. Yes, he's successful at what he does. Yes, he has a thriving studio with both the freedom and the responsibility that it entails. But, has it really changed Robert Olszewski, the young man who moved out to California twenty years ago with a new wife, an artistic talent, and a dream?

"I don't know why it is," Bob reflects today, "but in this country people seem to think you become a snob or something when you get suc-cessful. If the type of work we are doing here was easy, yes, it would be heady. But the work is so humbling in and of itself. I think maybe God gave me something that was so humbling, to make my living with, to keep me in order. I believe that," he insists. "I really do."

Bob grew up in the Pittsburgh, Pennsylvania, suburb of Natrona Heights, the son of a steelworker whose ancestors were Polish and Czechoslovakian. Bob was nine years old when his father died at the age of 43. It was during this sad time that Bob first recognized the frailty of human life, and developed a philo-

sophy of his own. "I became a risk-taker," he admits, "but not in a reckless way; I've tried to use my head. One of my favorite sayings, that I've lived by for years, is: 'This is not a dress rehearsal; this is it.' I've looked at things that way."

When the time came to think about going to college, Bob's mother and stepfather supported his decision to go, but there was very little money available to help. "I worked my way, building railroad cars and working in the steel mills," Bob explains. "For a year and a half, I worked full-time, saved my money, and went back." He graduated in 1968 from Indiana University of Pennsylvania with a degree in Art and English, and the credentials to teach.

The summer before, his future wife Linda had spent six weeks visiting relatives in California. When she came back, the couple discussed the possibilities of moving there. "I was showing my paintings in the best galleries in Pittsburgh at the time," Bob recalls, "and I knew I couldn't make a living selling paintings to steel-workers. I just could not see that as a possibility, so I knew I had to leave. I was either going to live outside of New York, Chicago or Los Angeles because they were the three major art centers in the country."

The following year Bob and Linda "graduated from college on a Thursday, got married on Saturday, and left for California on Monday morning," as Bob remembers now. "What a shock that was," he remarks, with an irrepressible grin. "I went from being a bachelor to a married college graduate, and moving out here, a cultural shock."

They settled in Camarillo, bought the house Bob still lives in today, and Bob began his dual career, teaching art at the junior high level and continuing the painting he had begun back in Pennsylvania. "Of the 365 days in a year," Bob says, "I bet I painted at least 340 of them."

> *"I think maybe God gave me something that was so humbling, to make my living with, to keep me in order."*

In 1972 Bob was "doing paintings and shipping them around to galleries and exhibitions," when the possibility of miniatures as an art form first occurred to him. One of the paintings he had on exhibition at the time was in a gallery in Las Vegas. "Someone broke into the gallery," he explains, "and stole three paintings." One of the three was Bob's. "The police asked me for a photograph of this work so that they could do an investigation," Bob recalls. "The canvases I was using at that time were about three feet by three feet. Usually I photograph everything I've done,

but this time I hadn't, so I sat down and from memory, did a reproduction of this piece small enough to put into an envelope."

The miniature painting, he decided, was really as good as the larger one. "What I realized when I looked at this small work was that the value of the work was not determined by its size. At this point," he remembers, "I was not really interested in miniatures as such, but I was really struck by this."

Bob also recognized the value of miniaturization as a teaching tool and began to "scale down my projects in the classroom because the value of the learning was just the same. I think you learn at a faster rate, in fact," he believes, "because each project has a beginning, a middle, and an end, in a shorter space of time."

The interest in miniaturization then carried over into his family life, in the form of a dollhouse for his daughter, Meredith. "The natural thing for a good, old Dad to do was to build her a dollhouse," he laughs. It was the first of only four Olszewski dollhouses ever built. "When the lady across the street saw it," Bob recalls, "she asked if I would build her one just like

This miniature room (above) was first used as a display for Bob's figurines at miniatures shows. "I was an avid minia-turist," he admits. "First I did all the miniature stuff, and then I got into figurines." Bob later copied the bookcase in this room in his full-size bedroom.

Bob stands before a painting (left) he did of the house he grew up in; Bob's father sits alone on the front steps. "He built this house with the help of his in-laws," Bob explains. "And when I moved out here, I realized that I would never be able to build a house. What a wonderful thing he did! This painting is just a very special reminder for me." Although he didn't build his home, he has made it very much his own. The bedroom (below left) features bookcases he built himself. Bob has also done much work on the outside of his home. His back yard (opposite page) is a favorite spot because "it's open and yet private," Bob says, adding, "I landscaped it, put the rocks in, and planted that tree. I moved tons of material back there, and laid the bricks in the patio."

it," so he did. And, then built two more, selling each one for $1,350. "We were broke at the time," Bob insists, "absolutely broke. I wasn't teaching summer school; I was spending all this time painting." Their second child was expected and "for some reason, our school insurance policy didn't cover a Caesarian section delivery, so that's what I used the money for," Bob says simply.

"I built these dollhouses and learned a lot, really fell in love with miniatures," he continues. There were built-in bookcases in each house and when Bob was looking for miniature figurines to put into Meredith's dollhouse, he found there was not much available in the quality he was looking for. "I realized that if I could

come up with a way to do fine miniature figurines, there might be some interest out there.

"Even with my background in the arts, I couldn't come up with a technique that would give me the kind of quality and detail I was looking for," Bob continues, until a chance conversation with a neighbor who practiced dentistry.

"We got to talking about carving teeth out of wax and casting them," Bob recalls. "I said, you mean to tell me that I can take a piece of wax and carve anything I want, and cast it and make molds? I was just....you could have peeled me off the ceiling!"

The excitement Bob felt that summer afternoon in 1977 was sustained when, a few months later, he carved

his first miniature figurine "with a nail and a screwdriver," sitting at a workbench in his garage, and developed the basics of the techniques he still uses today. "I had never carved before, in miniature. I thought it was the most beautiful thing in the world," he admits.

His enthusiasm, however, was not shared by the owners of several miniatures shops he contacted shortly after, trying to sell these new figurines. "Nobody wanted to talk to me," he recalls with chagrin. "So, I started to do the miniature show circuit," successfully. In the next fourteen months his gross sales were in the low six figures. "I was a one-man band," Bob laughs, "making and carving and painting in my home, and then doing all these shows, selling wholesale and retail."

Before the beginning of the next school year, Bob had an opportunity to become an artist full-time. When he told the principal of the school where he was teaching about his success with the miniature figurines, he said, as Bob recalls it now, "What are you coming back here for? Take a leave for a year; I'll guarantee your job."

Bob decided to take the principal up on his offer, even though "I didn't even know if I could paint this many things, let alone sell them," he insists. "I didn't have any studio to work in, so I took the doors off my bedroom closet and that's where I worked." His most successful pieces at that time were miniature copies of Hummel and Royal Doulton figurines, and he did not realize that it might be against the law to copy them.

When he was told by fellow artisans that he might be in legal trouble, "I was scared to death," Bob recalls. He decided to write to both companies to explain what he was doing. "I told them what I had done, explained to them how the whole miniature industry was based on taking large things and reducing them, told them how many I had sold and what I had sold them for," he remembers now, "and I told them if they asked me to stop, I would stop." He also sent each company examples of the work he was doing. And then, Bob waited.

Three or four months went by before he had a response to his letters, "and I was starting to get really scared," Bob recalls, when the first letter came from overseas. It was a 7-page contract from the Royal Doulton factory in England, "licensing me to do all of their figurines in miniature," he relates, "and I was absolutely stunned." A week later,

"I got another overseas letter in the mailbox, only this was very thin, short and to the point. It was from Mr. Goebel who owns the company that makes the Hummel figurines," Bob notes, adding that the letter requested a meeting.

"What I realized when I looked at this small work was that the value of the work was not determined by its size."

That meeting took place when both the president and vice president of Goebel, North America, arrived at Bob's home to review "the entire operation," Bob can recall calmly now. "At that time, I had hair down to here," he continues, indicating shoulder-length, "and a full beard. We don't have a formal dining room, so we are sitting at the kitchen table having lunch and I am trying to delay,

trying to build some kind of rapport with them."

When it was impossible to delay any longer, Bob escorted the two gentlemen to his closet studio. "It was hilarious," he will admit today, "the three of us standing in my closet." Bob pointed out his "carving department", his "research and development area," which was four books on a shelf, and, leaning against a nearby dresser, added that "this is our warehouse. We ship out of the bottom drawer. And they were fantastic. When they left, they offered me a contract as master artist. An interesting afternoon," he notes, and one which changed his life.

"When they offered me the contract," Bob continues, "the first problem was: would I be able to take my skills and train other people to do this kind of work, or were these skills so unique that only one man could have them." Remembering that he had been a teacher for eleven years, "and I had taught over 6,000 students in those eleven years," Bob explains, "I thought that if anyone could have a shot at training people, I

could do it.''

Although he had confidence in his abilities as a teacher, Bob thought about the contract for several months before accepting it ''because I knew it was going to change my life,'' he says. ''I didn't know what would happen, but I knew it was not going to be the same. I also remember thinking, during that time, about what my motivation would be to do it. What did I feel I was going to accomplish.''

Bob realized then that one of the major things he could accomplish was to bring an awareness of the miniatures world as a whole to many, many more people than he ever could on his own. With a company such as Goebel behind him, with its fine, worldwide reputation for quality, he ''could make a contribution to American art. Not too many people are in the kind of position to be able to do that,'' he believes. ''Shouldn't I, with an opportunity like this,'' he answered, ''try, at least try?''

Like many other ventures before and since, Goebel Miniatures Studios started with Bob's determination and his belief in his own artistic ability. He accepted the Goebel contract, and in January 1980, ''we moved into this building,'' he continues. ''There was not a wall in the place. We started from scratch. We had no market, no designs, few employees. I started out with four part-time people. I literally threw myself into this,'' Bob recalls, and for a time, did all the jobs himself, taking out the trash, working on new designs, and everything in between.

> ''I'm . . . trying to breathe life into something that stands only an inch tall. It's hard to do.''

The hours were long at the beginning, to be expected with this new venture, as Bob began building a staff of skilled artisans, and training them, and gradually, ''as each person here learned their craft, that allowed me to step back and live like a human being again,'' he explains.

''I've spent the last seven years laying the foundations for the Studios,'' Bob comments, and at the same time, has gradually re-established a normal home life. It was about four years ago that Bob and Linda agreed to divorce. Bob has since taken over the house and become a bachelor father to his two children. It has turned out to be a satisfactory arrangement for all of them. ''Linda is a great lady,'' Bob asserts. ''We just have very different ways, I guess.''

Now Bob prefers not to work evenings and weekends any longer, tries to schedule fewer business trips, ''because my kids will only be this age once, and I'm not going to miss it,'' he insists. The home he shares with them is comfortable and attractive, with many good memories for Bob. ''I'm a very visual person,'' he observes, walking through the house, ''so I make my home a visual statement of me.''

Many of his earlier paintings hang in the house, examples of specific milestones in his life. Some of these paintings had been sold and Bob has since bought them back. The one hanging in

the entry hall, reminiscent in some ways of Andrew Wyeth in its stark detail, is of the house in Pennsylvania where Bob grew up. His father sits alone on the porch in front. "He built that house with the help of his in-laws," Bob explains. "And when I moved out here, I realized that I would never be able to build a house. What a wonderful thing he did! We lived out in the country, and I think the real foundations of who I am came from living in that house, out in the country. It was a very, very happy time for me, a very special time." And he adds, pointing out the clouds he painted against a clear blue sky, "there's a fleetingness to them, like his life was. It is just a very special reminder for me."

Other Olszewski paintings hang on the walls in the living room, along with a display case containing each of Bob's miniature figurine designs to date. They are a visual record of his transition from painter to sculptor. "That was a difficult transition to make," Bob realizes now. "A painter thinks, surface, the surface of the work. Now I'm thinking, movement. I'm designing for visual clarity and emotion, trying to breathe life into something that stands only an inch tall. It's hard to do."

Just as Bob has successfully made the transition from painter to sculptor, he has also achieved his goal of passing his skills on to the people who have joined him in Goebel Miniatures Studios. "I love this studio so much," he insists. "This studio is an extension of myself. That is what it's about." Every step in the process of creating each miniature figurine is within Bob's control from its inception to its completion. "My name is on the work," he states, "and it's going to be the best of the best it can be."

A tour of Goebel Miniatures Studios starts in Bob's office, a space divided by a partition. On one side is his business desk and on the other is the heart of the operation, the work area where he carves the originals and paints the masters. "My title in the studio is Master Artist," Bob explains, "and that is not a title of arrogance, it just means I design and

Today Bob's work is done in this studio (opposite page), the domain of the Master Artist of Goebel Miniatures. The work surface extends around three sides of the room; the fourth wall is bookshelves. Although he is most well-known for his miniature sculptures, Bob has done other miniature work as well, including the dollhouse (top right) built for his daughter Meredith. He later built and sold three others similar to it. Pictured above and at right is a miniature porcelain studio. "I didn't build this," Bob explains. "This one I modified. It's like a miniature porcelain studio. The sign outside reads: "Olszewski Studios, Established 1977." A friend had built the structure and most of the furniture. "He was going to throw it away, and I said, no, give it to me. So I would carry this to the shows and have Olszewski Studios sitting on my table."

carve the masters. That's where the term comes from.''

An original design carved from wax is nearing completion this day and Bob explains how the ''lost wax'' process works: ''Once the piece is carved, we put a metal pipe over it and pour plaster over the piece. That is put into an oven overnight, and the temperature is gradually raised to 1400 degrees. All of the wax will drip out, leaving a hollow cavity inside the plaster. Into that you pour sterling silver and put it into water which dissolves the plaster, leaving the sterling figure. The next step is to encase the sterling in latex or rubber molds and put that in a mold press for several hours. You end up with a solid block of rubber around the piece. Next you very carefully cut the rubber mold apart, remove the sterling, and close it up again. And into this you squeeze wax. These wax forms are mounted on what is called a wax tree, a metal pipe is put over it, and plaster is poured in. Then into the oven again

and the wax drips out. Then, finally, you cast bronze. This is what the pieces are, hand-painted bronze.''

> ''The first problem was: would I be able to take my skill and train other people to do this kind of work, or were these skills so unique that only one man could have them?''

The hand-painting of each piece is even more intricate and technically demanding, starting with Bob's original carving. ''The whole time I'm carving, I'm thinking about what the piece is going to look like,'' he notes. ''I do all the original painting and I paint it just like a painting. I don't worry about production, I just make it look beautiful.''

Once the piece is completed to

Bob's satisfaction, two of his co-workers join him for the next step. ''On my left is a colorist who sits here and does nothing but match my colors. Then, on my right, is what we call a specialist, the person who is going to see this piece through the studio. She writes down the sequence as I do the painting.'' The object of this attention is a row of perhaps half a dozen bronze figures, all alike, mounted on a wood stick.

''I will do a stick and the specialist will do a stick,'' Bob explains. ''What I focus on is the look, how the piece looks. Does it look beautiful enough? Her role is to ensure that the production people will understand this.'' The sequence of steps in which each piece will be painted is gone over many times before each new piece is put into production. It is a painstaking and necessary process, Bob believes, ''and when I'm certain they understand it, then they can start production on it.'' As each tray of figurines is completed, they are brought back to

Three display cases (opposite page) hanging on the wall in Bob's living room represent his work from the beginning through the end of 1986. Closeups of the three groupings are shown on this page. Some of the pieces are no longer being made, and some were never made in quantity. "In the first collection there were four reproductions out of five," Bob points out. "This was my first original," a sparrow with flowers, shown at the lower left in the photo at top left.

Bob for further scrutiny. And, finally, they are shipped out to collectors and shops all over the country, a handcrafted product from beginning to end.

Bob feels a certain sense of sadness and anger when he hears the question: "Are these mass-produced?" Only a few people know the long hours that he has spent training the staff who works with him, the long hours each one of the staff has spent becoming exceedingly proficient at what he or she does. "Sure I work hard," Bob admits, "because I love what I do. But these people in the

> **"I don't worry about production, I just make it look beautiful."**

studio, I care for them so much. I cannot tell you how special these people are to me. They work so hard for us, and they deliver so consistently. They deliver quality every single day. I think that's what this is about, and I think that is what makes hand-done work what it is. I'm truly offended when people doubt it."

So Bob tries very hard to ignore his critics, and there really isn't much free time to think about them, anyway. "We have only begun," Bob says about the work still to do. "The heart of this business will be the original work," and there are many projects in the progress that are already challenging Bob's creativity. "I think it's going to be a great, great adventure," he says with a broad smile, the smile of a man who is happy and fulfilled, an artist who has realized his dream.

A visit to Goebel Miniatures Studios

PHOTO 1: Bronzing

PHOTO 2: The first grinding

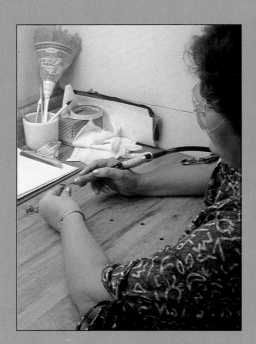

PHOTO 3 (left): The second grinding
PHOTO 4 (above): Coloration

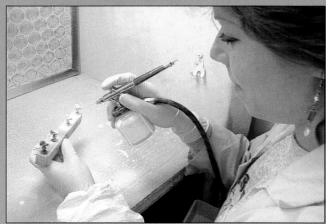

PHOTO 5: Air brushing the primer

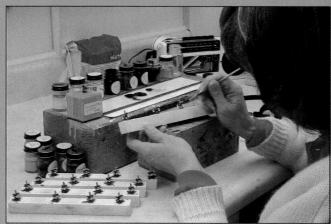

PHOTO 6: Glazing

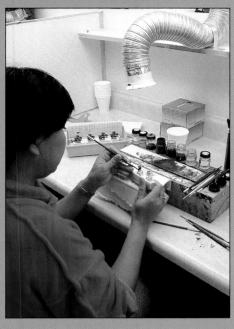

PHOTO 7 (left): Glazing
PHOTO 8 (above): The glazing department

PHOTO 9 (above): Painting features
PHOTO 10 (right): Detailing features

PHOTO 11 (above): The features department
PHOTO 12: Doing touch-up work

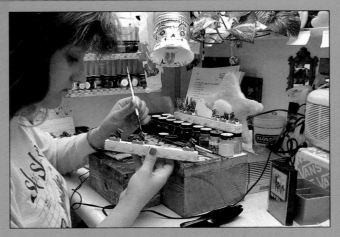

PHOTO 13 (above): Touch-up
PHOTO 14 (right): Sample painting

PHOTO 15: Air brushing the final glaze

PHOTO 16: The art director

PHOTO 17: Goebel Miniatures on display in the Studios' lobby.

*Victorian square grand piano by Ralph Partelow; vase by Pete Acquisto;
flowers by Marjorie Meyer; paintings by Marjorie Adams.*

Ralph Partelow, Jr.

Just as my fingers on these keys
Make music, so the self-same sounds
On my spirit make a music, too.
—*Wallace Stevens*

Very often there is a single thread that creates the strongest part of the fabric of one's life. For Ralph E. Partelow, Jr., that thread has been linked irrevocably to the piano. "I have had a love affair with the piano for as long as I can remember," he insists.

"There is nothing like it," he feels, "growing up with music in the home." His grandmother played the piano, his mother played, and 30 years ago at the age of 10, Ralph decided he must, too. "My mother played by ear; she never learned to read music," Ralph recalls. "But she wanted me to learn,

and I wanted to learn."

Growing up in Eastern New York State, Ralph remembers that his father, a house painter by vocation, took him along sometimes, when he worked. "I was about 9 or 10. He would paint churches sometimes, and I would go with him, help him with this or that. There would be a piano or an organ, and I would just love to play it," Ralph reminisces. It wasn't long before his parents realized that Ralph might have some musical ability, and bought him a piano, "an old upright, and I was enthralled," he relates.

It was during school shop classes, when he was 12, that Ralph built his

Ralph Partelow is shown on the opposite page holding the first miniature piano he ever made, and a more recent one. Pictured above him is the station in Kenya where the Partelows are currently serving as missionaries. (Photo by Ralph Partelow). Examples of some of his work shown on this page are two harps in one-inch and half-inch scales (above left) and the Steinway Deluxe Concert Grand (above right), with the interior detail pictured at right.

first miniature piano. "I just wanted to make a piano, and I was eccentric about it," he confesses. "My parents thought I was crazy." But his father bought Ralph some simple tools, and he used his father's discarded single-edge razor blades to do the hand-carving. "That's how it began," he says simply.

When he was 14 years old, Ralph had his first, formal piano lessons, with Florence Cavanagh, a retired Pawling, New York, church musician, who gave him her own grand piano shortly thereafter. "I was so proud of that thing," Ralph remembers. Two years later his instructor was a retired concert pianist whose own stu-

dent-instructor relationship could be traced back through Franz Liszt to Beethoven. "I had no idea what music was all about until I met Earyle Browne," Ralph insists. "I took lessons from him for two or three years, and that was an experience I shall never forget."

The Browne home was filled with elegant, European antique furniture, including a jeweled ebony music cabinet with gold overlay said to have once belonged to Marie Antoinette. It

stood next to the 7-foot Steinway grand piano where Ralph took his lessons. "Earyle Browne introduced me not only to another way of life," Ralph believes, "but he also took me down to New York City and introduced me to the Steinway people, took me around New York on music-buying trips. When I was taking a music lesson, he'd walk all over this big house, even out to his rose garden, and when he'd hear a mistake, he would yell at the top of his lungs,

'Play it again.' He'd know exactly where I made the mistake,'' Ralph marvels, adding that he also remembers the ruler Mr. Browne kept on the piano, ''and he'd use it, on your fingers! I used to go and take a music lesson with absolute fear,'' he admits, ''but he was the best teacher you could ever imagine. He was well-known and well-respected. I think it was because he was so strict.''

Although he took his music lessons very seriously, Ralph was not as conscientious about his regular schoolwork. ''I almost quit school in my senior year,'' he confesses. I just didn't want to go to school. I hated it.'' But his mother would not let him give up, so Ralph graduated from high school in 1964 and went to work for the Foundation of Christian Living, publishers of the Reverend Norman Vincent Peale's sermons, sister to the popular *Guideposts* magazine.

Just over a year later, Ralph applied for admittance to Nyack College, an interdenominational Christian school in Nyack, New York, intending to major in music. ''It was a wonder they ever accepted me with my grades,'' he believes, ''but they did, on probation,'' to start in the winter semester. It was November 1965, the height of the Vietnam War, and Ralph, like many other young men, received a draft notice. He had three weeks to get his affairs in order, to adjust to the fact that he would very likely have to go to Vietnam, ''and we all struggled with that,'' he remembers, ''the family struggled with it. But I had to go.''

Ralph was sent by train up to the induction center in Albany where he was to have a physical examination. ''The doctor checked me over and said, 'You have a heart murmur; you're not going anywhere,' '' as Ralph recalls the incident now. ''I just

The Partelows' African house (left, top) is in Machakos, a rural town an hour and a half southeast of Nairobi. Ralph teaches African nationals in Kenya, East Africa (left), where some of them will be ministers or pastors and others will work in Christian education. Although he does not serve as a pastor, he sometimes preaches in churches there (left, center).

Ralph, Carolyn and Jonathan Partelow were at home in Littleton, Colorado, when the photograph at right was taken. Their love for Africa is reflected in the books (above) and art in their home. Always interested in miniatures, Ralph visited Madurodam, a miniature village in Holland (below right).

couldn't believe it.'' He had recently had a physical exam as part of his college entrance application which had turned up no problem. ''I went to a heart specialist the next week, and he found nothing wrong with me,'' Ralph continues. ''And I just wonder. It's as if the Lord was saying: 'I gave you one chance; don't blow it again.' ''

The Ralph Partelow who entered Nyack College in January of 1966 was a very shy, young man, the kind of person for whom public speaking was completely out of the question. He would communicate instead through his music. ''No way was I ever going to be a preacher,'' he decided then. Shortly before his second year of college, he was to change his mind.

''You've probably heard people saying they have a 'call' to the ministry, or something like that,'' Ralph comments. ''I often wondered what that was. Is it conscience? What is it?'' He found the answer in his Bible. ''I was reading in Exodus about the 'call' of Moses,'' Ralph recalls. ''Moses was shy, he was afraid, and he gave God one excuse after another why he couldn't lead his people into Israel. As

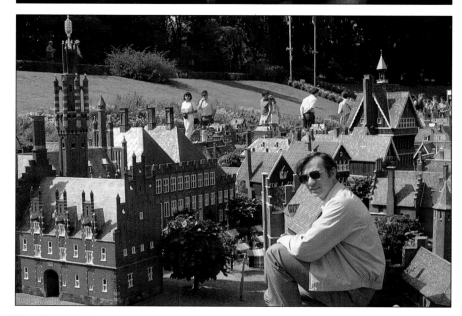

I read that, I just felt that the Lord was speaking to me through that whole episode. I felt that if the Lord could use somebody like Moses, He could certainly use somebody like me, if He wanted me. I just felt an inner peace when I made the decision to change from music to theology. It's as simple as that.''

That ''inner peace'' sustained Ralph when he enrolled in his first speech class. ''I had to take what they call homiletics,'' he explains, ''the art of preaching. The funny thing is that the very thing I feared most when I went into college, homiletics, is now what I teach. Sometimes the very thing that you're afraid of is what you're really qualified

to do,'' he believes. ''It's interesting.''

The young lady Ralph met at about this same time had no doubt about what she wanted to do. Carolyn Kline had grown up in Ohio, west of Cleveland, and enrolled at Nyack College as an English major, ''but I never really wanted to teach,'' she recalls now. ''I never really wanted to be anything except a pastor's wife, which was ridiculous because I didn't even know a pastor at that point. But I felt, from the time I was a junior in high school, that was what I was going to be.''

Ralph and Carolyn were married on September 1, 1968, mid-way through their college years. It was slightly less than a year later that Carolyn

began experiencing the symptoms that would be diagnosed as multiple sclerosis, a numbness in her feet and legs. ''I was doing office work at Xerox Corporation at the time,'' she recalls, ''and I thought I had a pinched nerve or something in my back, but when the numbness started creeping upwards, and not very slowly, I decided that there was something more to it.''

After the first doctor they consulted could not find the cause of her numbness, Carolyn was referred to a neurologist ''who, as it turned out, was the President of the Hudson Valley chapter of the MS Society,'' she continues. ''So he knew when he saw me walk in the door what I had; he could tell by my gait.''

A few months before, Ralph had been appointed the pastor of an inter-denominational church in New Jersey, not far from Nyack, and the couple was busy settling into the house provided for them by the church, when the MS became far worse. ''By the first week in January 1970,'' Ralph explains, ''she was completely paralyzed.'' The doctors, some of the best neurologists on the East Coast at the time, held out very little hope for any kind of recovery at all. ''But in six weeks,'' Ralph continues, ''she walked out of the hospital without a limp.''

For Carolyn, those six weeks were a very positive experience in her life. With steroid treatments, ''I was able to see some kind of improvement every single day,'' she recalls. ''I really enjoyed being in the hospital for those six weeks because I really felt God so close to me, and knew that He loved me so much.''

In the years since, Carolyn has coped

Shown in the photo at left, above, are an 18th century walnut clavichord and an 18th century cherry harpsichord. Both pieces are half-inch scale, as are the spinet, baby grand and upright pianos at left. Half-inch scale pianos account for about 10% of the pianos Ralph creates. One of his most popular pianos is the Louis XV upright, built of walnut in one-inch scale, pictured on the opposite page, above. Below it is shown a colonial church organ, painted white with mahogany detailing.

with MS through a variety of treatments, remission and relapses, to its present stage, chronic progressive. "I went through a lot of different things," she explains, adding with an irrepressible grin, "but I never lost my speech!"

Because of the MS, as well as other complications, Ralph and Carolyn were told "there was no possibility of a child being born, ever," Ralph comments, but Jonathan Edward Partelow celebrated his 13th birthday in August 1987. Jonathan has an African nickname which means "loved one," because the African nationals the Partelows were working with "knew that he was a special child to us," Ralph explains.

Ralph, Carolyn and Jonathan have been going to Africa as missionaries since 1978. In fact, the pianos Ralph makes have helped finance his missionary training over the years. He views his miniatures work as part of God's provision for his material needs as a missionary.

> *"Sometimes the very thing that you're afraid of is what you're really qualified to do."*

In 1986 Ralph earned a Master of Divinity degree from Denver Seminary, where he is presently enrolled in the Doctor of Ministry program.

"A lot of people think we're nuts for even trying to go back to Africa," Ralph admitted as they planned their third trip for missionary service there with Africa Inland Mission to teach at Scott Theological College. "But I really feel that the quality of life is worth a lot more than the quantity of it. It's true Carolyn can't do some things, but she does more than a lot of people in her condition. She has a gift for linguistics; I haven't got that ability. She is able to communicate much better than I am in Swahili. She's a real blessing to the students who come to visit her, in a different way than I would be," he believes.

Ralph and Carolyn are sitting in the living room of their Denver home as he talks about the family's plans for the next few years, and recalls the events of their life together. A 6-foot Steinway parlor grand piano fills one end of the handsome room. At the other is a glass-fronted cabinet full of miniature pianos, most of them examples of the pianos Ralph makes now.

Not among this collection is the piano Ralph made for Carolyn while they were dating in college. "It's awful, compared to what he makes now," she insists. "But at the time,

it was wonderful. Everyone thought so. But, it was not at all in scale and the finish was wretched. Of course," she laughs, "the only reason the finishes are any good is because I got into it."

Although Ralph had been making miniature pianos since he was a young boy, he notes that "if I'm going to find a starting point for this business, it was in 1976." That was the year they decided to build and furnish a dollhouse as an anniversary gift for Carolyn's parents. A piano, of course, was one of the pieces of furniture Ralph built for the house. "Some-body saw it," he recalls, and suggest-ed that Ralph show it to a shop own-er, with surprising results. "I'll buy anything you make," Ralph now recalls her saying.

At the same time, Carolyn was read-ing a book about dollhouses she had ordered from a book club. "Two names came up so often in that book," she remembers, "Marian O'Brien and Ellen Blauer. I told him to write to these two people, and he didn't want to. He was very reluc-tant." When he finally did, the response they received gave Ralph and Carolyn the encouragement they needed to pursue their dream of some-day doing missionary work.

"Marian O'Brien was our first real customer, for a piano," Ralph recalls, "and she said I could sell as many as I could make, and that really encour-aged me." He and Carolyn had want-ed to resign from the church where Ralph was then the pastor, "go back to school, and hopefully, go overseas somewhere in mission work," he ex-plains. Building and selling miniature pianos could provide the necessary in-come, they decided.

> "I really feel that
> the quality of life is
> worth a lot more
> than the quantity
> of it."

Ralph had learned as a teenager that Steinway & Sons builds a super-ior piano, and he has owned three of them himself. So, "when I began to think about doing pianos full-time, I wrote to the Steinway Company and asked if they had any pictures or a catalog, anything I could borrow and use," Ralph recalls. "Lo and behold, John Steinway himself wrote back to me and said, 'I am a fellow miniatur-ist.'" Ralph received a box full of helpful information shortly thereafter, and in July, 1977, he and Carolyn had a tour of the factory, at John Stein-way's invitation. "Every chance I get, I put in a plug for Steinway," Ralph comments, "because it is a handmade piano. Even today."

While they were there, John Stein-way gave Ralph a very special gift, a miniature piano that he had made. "It is a real Steinway, made by Steinway," Ralph points out, "and I'm just as honored and thrilled as can be. The same scale that I make, and he's only made a few, one for Van Cliburne, one for Skitch Henderson, a few to others, and he gave me one."

Ralph has kept in touch with John Steinway over the years, has occa-sionally sent him miniatures supplies, and on his most recent trip to Denver before the Partelows left for Africa, Steinway was introduced to Jonathan and heard him play the piano. "He signed one of Jonathan's music books," Carolyn mentions. "Jonathan was so proud of that." Ralph is equally proud of the inscription on the bottom of his miniature Steinway: "Given to Ralph Partelow by John Steinway, July 6, 1977, with renewed friendship and respect." The miniature was un-signed when Ralph first received it, "but I sent it back to him later and asked him to sign it," Ralph explains, holding the piano so he can demon-strate how it comes apart.

"He's made this like a real piano," Ralph points out. His own early pian-os did not have some of the realistic detail they have today — hand-carved wood keys, for instance. Ralph cred-its a collector in Nebraska for "insist-ing on my making wooden keys, and I have never gone back to the paper keys" used at first. "And Ellen Blauer. I never told her this, but she suggested putting a hole in the lid so the stick would stay up," he recalls. "A lot of our customers have suggest-ed little things," Ralph says, adding that the pianos have always been sold with the guarantee that they can be re-turned should there be any need for repairs.

Ralph recalls that one woman called to tell him her son had been sleepwalk-ing and had run into a cabinet full of miniatures. "All the stuff in that cabi-net, including three pianos, fell off and broke," he was told, "and we fixed all three. Just funny things happen." Not surprising when one realizes that there are some 1,500 Partelow crea-tions in existence today.

The musical instruments Ralph has made over the years have ranged through several centuries and include both replicas of museum pieces as well as likenesses such as a simple, French harpsichord. There are Stein-ways, of course. "I told Mr. Stein-way that I would not put 'Steinway' on any piano that was not a replica," Ralph explains. "These are the Stein-way specifications," Ralph says, pointing to the full-size drawings on the wall behind his workbench. "That cross-section of a piano has been a great help to me."

It takes Ralph about two weeks to complete a piano, but there are usual-ly half a dozen of them in various stages of completion in his workshop at any given time. Stacks of walnut, rosewood, mahogany and cherry sit at one end of his work area. "The black pianos are made of cherry because of its tight grain," Ralph comments. "It makes the finish better."

Finishing each piano requires up to 12 coats of varnish, sanded between each coat. "It depends on the kind of wood," Ralph explains about the number of coats required. "Mahogany will take more than cherry, for instance." If a replica piano is to have a painting on the lid, that part is sent to the Partelows' longtime friend, Mildred Schneider, before any assembling or finishing is done. She has produced the artwork on almost all of those Partelow pianos. "It has worked out well," Ralph believes. "She knows just the texture of the wood. We really appreciate Mildred not only for her talent, but also because we can rely on her."

Almost every Partelow piano is made by special order, so although Ralph may not know his collectors personally, he does know where each piano has been sent. "I keep records on everything," he admits. "I've just got reams of these records and they are virtually of no use except that I know where all the pianos went." Since the record is in chronological order, it also shows the periods of time when they didn't make any pianos at all.

"When we left for Kenya in late 1978, the first trip," Ralph recalls, "I suggested to my Dad that they try to make some miniatures. I said, why don't you make pianos while I'm gone in Africa, so we taught them how to make three or four or five instruments, and they did pretty well," he feels. "They were well-respected for their work. Then Dad decided that it wasn't a good idea for me to come back and make miniatures, and he make them, too. So they didn't make them anymore."

Now Ralph's parents are getting back into miniatures again, "and they're very excited about it," Ralph observes. "It gives us something in common. They encouraged me when I was young, and I just feel that now is the time to encourage them." It is a

situation not everyone is aware of, as Carolyn points out. "Some people in the miniature world actually were angry with us because they thought Ralph took away his father's business, which he didn't! His father didn't teach him how to do it, Ralph taught his father how to do it."

When Ralph thinks back to his childhood, "creativity seems to be the bottom line," he believes. "Both my parents were creative, and we grew up with that atmosphere. I credit any creativity I have with the childhood that I had." Today, Ralph says, "I like the balance between the mental energy that I spend on studies and teaching, and the creative part which is enjoyable. Miniatures are a release," he feels. And Carolyn adds with the assurance of an observant

The photo on the opposite page shows a significant piano for the Partelows — their 1500th instrument, a 17th century French spinet harpsichord with decorative painting by Mildred Schneider, who also decorated the 17th century Italian harpsichord made of rosewood shown above.

wife, "To understand Ralph thoroughly, you've got to understand that he's got to be *too busy* to be happy. And I do mean, too busy. There are just not enough hours in the day for a normal person to get done all the things he gets done, but somehow, he gets it all done."

Still, he has time to sit at his Steinway and create beautiful music. The piano, in full-size or in miniature, is a strong thread in the fabric of Ralph E. Partelow, Jr.'s life.

A visit to the Partelow workshop

PHOTO 1: Ralph is carving a Chippendale piano leg.

PHOTO 2: He is putting the finishing touches on the carved leg.

PHOTO 3: He fits the carved Chippendale leg on the piano case.

PHOTO 4: Ralph signs, dates and codes the bottom side of a piano case.

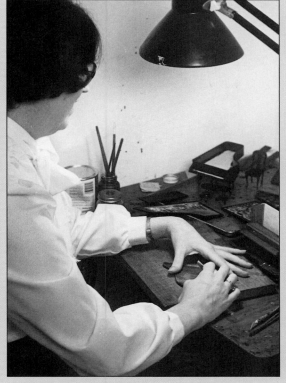

PHOTO 5: Carolyn sands piano parts for finishing before the pianos are assembled.

PHOTO 6 (above): Ralph is assembling a grand piano.

PHOTO 7: Carolyn is sanding a Queen Anne baby grand in the finishing process, which requires a minimum of ten coats.

PHOTO 8 (below): He is holding a completed Chippendale grand piano next to an unfinished one.

Marty Saunders

Art flourishes where there is a sense of adventure.
—Alfred North Whitehead

"What I'm interested in— what I really love—is what I'm working on today," Marty Saunders states unequivocally, seated in the enclosed sunporch of her home in Hingham, Massachusetts, to talk about her life and work. This immediacy, this enthusiasm for what she does is as much a part of her genetic makeup as is her bone structure or her sparkling blue eyes. Marty Saunders did not become the widely-acclaimed doll artist that she is overnight.

Born in St. Louis, Missouri, to an American father and a Canadian mother "who had known each other all their lives," Marty had, by some standards, a rather unorthodox and peripatetic childhood. "My American grandfather had five houses in Kingsville, Ontario," she relates, "and they ranged from summer cottage type things to very elaborate," so Marty's mother who "came to the United States and hated it, loathed it," Marty continues, could have the

use of whichever house might be available during the summer, as well as at other times of the year. Marty, of course, was taken along.

Her father owned limestone quarries in the Midwest, and "because my father's business was seasonal, we had a house in Illinois, and a house in Key West, and in Fort Lauderdale," Marty remembers.

> *"By the time I was five, I was making dolls.*

It was in Florida that Marty had the only substantial formal schooling of her younger years. Her mother considered school "an inconvenience to her social life," Marty laughs, but one winter school officials did insist that Marty attend. "I spent three months in Dade County third grade and I had a wonderful time," Marty recalls. "It was great. Then some winters they would insist that we have a tutor. Florida was real tough about school."

But Florida offered opportunities that Marty's mother enjoyed. "My uncle had quite a boat," Marty remembers, "and he would bring it

through the Panama Canal in November and December, and then not use it for several months, so Mother had the use of it. She could get a group of friends together and cruise the Caribbean, and it was fun because it was big enough to take about twelve guests."

It was during this period that, Marty relates, "I met a lot of famous people in the world when I was a very young child, movie stars and fake Russian princes, interesting people. Clark Gable did impress me. He was a frequent visitor, a good friend of my uncle's." Another visitor, a New York decorator, brought Marty a doll she had bought at F.A.O. Schwartz because she had seen Marty "spending hours and hours, cutting out doll dresses and designing things." Marty recalls that the doll "had a plain, 1930's hairdo, so I could make wigs and hats. It was a flat enough hairdo to do all that sort of thing."

It was not Marty's first doll, of course. "My mother reminds me, when she wants to say what a horrible brat I was, of the baby doll with a handmade layette that she had made and gave me for my third birthday." Several months later, Marty's mother found her precocious

Marty Saunders converted a second floor bedroom in her Cape Cod-style house into a studio, complete with skylights and larger windows, overlooking the wildlife area behind the house. A respected painter, Marty insists that she paints "what I like to paint," adding, "and I'm funny about awards and things. They go into a drawer and I never want to see them. Somehow, they impede the work."

daughter cutting the layette apart "and resewing it because it was the wrong period," Marty laughs.

"By the time I was five, I was making dolls," she says. When Marty and her mother went to Canada to visit, "she had to take gifts," Marty explains, "and since she was the youngest of thirteen children, I had a hundred Canadian cousins. From the time I was five until I was eighteen, it was my job every year to make presents for them all." Sometimes they were rag dolls, "and then I'd do books of paper dolls, books of costumes, never meant to be cut out," Marty recalls. "I was horrified when they cut them out. These were meant to be books. This was historic!"

Marty had always been interested in history. "My father was crazy about history," Marty claims.

Marty is a collector as well as a creator, and her own work is displayed along with her collections. Antique porcelain cups and saucers and porcelain dolls (above) reside in a glass cabinet in her living room. On some of the shelves in this cabinet her own dolls are displayed (opposite page). A 3/4-inch scale dollhouse in her collection is also the subject of one of Marty's paintings (top).

"Every house we ever owned, except the ones in Florida, were always tremendously interesting, historically." Although Marty's father encouraged her interest in history, "he was dead set against my being an artist of

any kind," Marty insists. "He took my art supplies away from me whenever he could. He really felt that it was a foolish occupation." And this was in spite of the fact that Marty's grandfather "made his first million at thirteen by being an artist," she notes. He was apprenticed to a lithographer at the time, inventing and patenting a process to make colored labels for canned foods. "So, my grandfather loved and collected art," Marty continues. "My grandmother loved to paint. For her sixtieth birthday, she got a trip to Paris to study art. I mean, it wasn't that this thing came from nowhere," Marty asserts,

trying to understand her father's feelings.

During these early years, the years Marty and her mother were moving from house to house, Marty absorbed the art influences that would be with her all her life, the curiosity about history that continues today, like "an open sponge," she claims. "My children think I cheated them by making them go to school," she laughs. "They think that somehow you lose it, all this curiosity."

Marty did finally begin a formal education when, at the age of twelve, she moved with her mother to Santa Fe after her parents had divorced. "I started in high school," she recalls, "but there weren't any problems. It was fun to go to school because I had never really been to school before.

> *"My father...took my art supplies away from me whenever he could. He really felt that it was a foolish occupation."*

"Santa Fe was a good place for me," Marty recalls. "Everybody was an artist. At least, everybody I cared about was an artist." It was in the mid- to late 1940's, a time when many of the "people who are just now being recognized were young artists out there." One of them "took me on as his apprentice and I worked in the studio," Marty explains. She painted while he painted, "and he criticized and was helpful, and taught me how to look, how to see. Well, that was great fun, great fun," she recalls nostalgically.

It was the beginning of an intense interest in portraiture and sculpture. She learned to work with the native clays of New Mexico to do sculpture, firing her pieces the way the Indians did in a backyard kiln fired with dung. "But it wasn't fine enough," she says. "The clay was coarse, more like stoneware. Our ranch was next to the Santa Domingo pueblo and I knew a lot of the Indian women, but they were very hesitant to have anything to do with a white girl. I could see that they were polishing their pottery with pieces of bone, but every time I came near them, they would stop. So I missed something there, but not much, not much," she insists, laughing.

With this background, it was obvious that Marty would go to art school, and she hoped to enroll in the Art Students League in New York City, but her father insisted that she return to St. Louis and attend Washington University instead. "He didn't think New York City and the Art Students League was the proper place for a girl," Marty recalls.

"I became very disenchanted at art school," Marty admits. "Washington University's art school was deeply involved in German abstract expressionism at the time, and I was much more interested in portraiture and sculpture, very interested in sculpture." Marty remembers having "a very bad run-in" with one of the instructors, "and I objected to the head of the Art School" to no avail. So she turned her attention instead to academics. "I thought so many things were fascinating that I just kept going to school," she explains. When she reluctantly graduated in 1952, Marty had majors in art, history, English, psychology and education.

During her college years Marty lived with her father in St. Louis, not far from the Washington University campus, in one of what she terms his "historically interesting houses." Built in 1910 by Adolphus Busch for his mother, the mansion's master bathroom was plumbed to serve beer. "There were nine beer levers in that bathroom," Marty marvels, "so when she was dressing or whatever, she could just run whatever kind of beer she wanted. Then, under the staircase, was a marble room with a fountain and a fish that could be made to spurt champagne, beer, or water. I thought it was funky; I thought it was great fun," she recalls, "but my father didn't think it was so funny. He took them all out. I thought that was terrible because that was the charm of the house."

It was at Washington University that Marty met her future husband,

Masters in Miniature
113

Bill Saunders, "but we never had a date," she confesses. By the time they were married, "we had been best friends for years," Marty insists.

Marty went to Colorado after graduation to work for the Singer Sewing Machine Company, teaching sewing machine teachers how to teach, as she puts it, "and I hated it. My mother had worked for Singer and I had done some promotional material for them, designed some courses for them," so it seemed a logical job to take at the time.

It wasn't long, however, before she and Bill were married and moved to

Morristown, New Jersey, a close commute to Bill's engineering job in New York City. "He was one of the designers at Bell Labs working on the Nike missile," Marty explains, "and he held some of the important, early patents at the time." When the Korean War broke out, men such as Bill who had high security clearances were drafted but not sent overseas. "They called it the Four Eye Division," Marty recalls; "everybody had a Ph.D."

That division was sent to the Southwest, and Marty was able to go along. Their first daughter was born "at home, on my mother's ranch in

Built-in shelves (left) in a hallway between the living room and dining room contain room settings and the dolls Marty has created and kept in her own collection. On the opposite page is a portrait doll of Jebez Bowen, taken from a painting made by John Singleton Copley in 1762. With him in this setting is Marty's porcelain replica of Copley's "Unknown Lady," painted in 1761. (Photo by Anne Day Smith)

she confesses. "You didn't have the freedom to do what you wanted to do, in order to please the customer. And," she adds, "society children are very hard to paint. I saw an awful lot of wealthy, problem children. I really get upset when I see children who are neglected, abused, that sort of thing. I think, perhaps," Marty muses, "that I felt some child neglect myself, although I think I was lucky because the people that I picked out to be with me were fun and great and interesting and comfortable. But I saw some children who were in very sick situations, and I was very unhappy about that."

> *"I think I was lucky because the people that I picked out to be with me were fun and great and interesting and comfortable."*

New Mexico, which was kind of fun," Marty remembers. Another daughter and a son completed their family, "all born within three years," she says. "Going back to Santa Fe at that time was fun," Marty recalls, because she could renew earlier acquaintances, especially among the artists there.

"I think Morristown was a shock to me," she confesses. "When I was a young girl, everybody I knew was doing something. They weren't just playing bridge, or out to lunch, or any of those things. I didn't understand that; why weren't people making something or doing something?"

Did she consider herself somewhat unusual in that environment? "Oh, sure," she replies, matter of factly,

"but I had come to accept the fact that people who are artists are considered very different." She continued to paint, "but when the children were little, I was a mother, not a professional painter."

When her youngest child started school, Marty began "to seriously become a professional portrait painter." The Saunders family was living in Sherborne, Massachusetts, at that time, "a kind of social town and there wasn't any trouble getting commissions."

She continued doing portraits on commission for a number of years, until "I got tired of the difficult demands, and sometimes the loss of integrity in doing some portraits,"

It was time for new direction, and "by that time, I had met Betty Valentine," Marty continues. "We met in 1959. We had bought our house in Sherborne, and Betty and I took sailing lessons at the same time on a little lake there." Marty was driving an old Model A car with a somewhat recalcitrant gear box at that time, and after the lesson, "I accidentally put it in reverse and drove into the lake," Marty recalls with amusement. "She was standing there watching and she laughed her head off."

It turned out to be the beginning of a longlasting friendship. At that time, though, "I was intrigued by her sense of mechanical things," Marty believes, "because she decided she was going to get right in there and fix this thing for me.''

In her inimitable way, Marty asked Betty, ''what do you do?'' When she found that Betty made miniature furniture, Marty recalled seeing the Thorne Rooms when she was quite young, and again in her teens when an aunt who collected and documented antique French cottons took Marty to the Art Institute in Chicago. ''When I was in college,'' Marty recalls, ''several times she took me to the Art Institute with her, and I was allowed to play in the Thorne Rooms, the ones they didn't show, and get out boxes to examine all these things. I was totally in love with them,'' she admits.

When she visited Betty's home and saw ''this long, large bookcase filled with these pieces of furniture,'' Marty wanted to know, ''When are you going to put some human beings in this?'' Betty replied, Marty recalls now, ''When you make them, I'll do that.''

Although she considered herself primarily a portrait painter at the time, Marty had been making some portrait dolls of her children, for them to play with. ''I was very dissatisfied with the weight of the head, the texture of it all,'' she remembers, and Betty suggested that she make them of porcelain.

Still, it was over a dozen years later that Marty made her first miniature porcelain doll, and it was to settle a bet with, and as a gift for, Betty Valentine. ''I put that porcelain in my hand, and it was....well, great, terrific. I loved it!'' Marty remembers deciding, ''this is it; this is the stuff.''

The first doll Marty made, Betty's doll, was a portrait of Camille Monet taken from a painting in Boston's Museum of Art. Marty's second doll was started at the same time. ''I thought, why do just one,'' she explains, airily. ''The technique I was developing meant that the clay had to rest between stages. It needed to absorb more moisture. Since I had worked with clay all my life, I knew when it was too dry and when I could do what I needed to do to it.''

Those first dolls had bodies made of muslin and stuffed with kapok, ''but

they had no armature,'' Marty recalls. That came along when she discovered the longevity of stainless steel wire. Not pipe cleaners, ever.

> ''*I have not a competitive bone in my body.*''

''When you say pipe cleaners to me, I go through the ceiling,'' Marty insists, adding that her earlier art training had taught her that ''you did things in a workmanlike fashion because this is what you're leaving for posterity. Every material I use, I look at the longevity of it. If I'm using inferior material, then I'm giving

myself a lot of problems. So, ''she continues, ''I set up these sets of rules. When you're a dollmaker, you can make your own rules.''

One of Marty's rules is that ''the doll should last two hundred years,'' so the fabrics she uses are almost always new ones, even though the costumes are created in virtually the same way the originals would have been. ''I just love to research,'' Marty enthuses. ''I want the fabric to be right, I want the underwear to be right, and I want everything to be right. I get a big kick out of research.''

Marty also gets very enthusiastic about teaching others to make dolls. ''I was one of the first original people

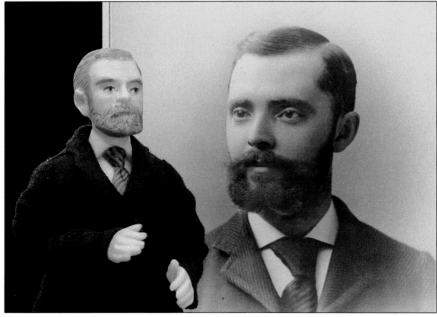

Marty attributes her ability to sculpt from photographs (left) to the fact that she has painted for years, and knows "what muscles are like." The two children on this page were copied from 19th century paintings. Of the one shown above left Marty explains, "I'm trying. . .here to sculpt the cat right on the arm."

to go to the I.G.M.A. School at Castine," she notes, "and I've been teaching there every year since. I have learned so much from my students. I've found that the most interesting things come out of people who have never touched clay, have never sculpted anything in their lives.

"The people who taught me the most in my whole life," she insists, "were those people who allowed me to go in my own direction. There are people who insist that you do everything their way, but how do you know it's the right way? How do I know it's the right way?" Her students, Marty observes, "come with their own set

of rules, their own ideas, and those are absolutely wonderful. I really enjoy teaching," she concludes.

Marty's teaching as well as many of her other artistic endeavors nearly came to an end on Memorial Day weekend in 1984. The car she was driving, on a quiet country road near her home, was struck violently by another vehicle, causing Marty to receive a severe head injury. The recuperation period has been long and difficult; in fact, it is still going on, three years later. But her strength and determination have allowed her to do battle with the limitations on her body and to make the adjustments

necessary to continue her work and as normal a life as possible.

Because of the aftermath of that accident, Marty has to perform even everyday tasks by keeping her head erect, by never bending over. "All the things you take for granted in life," she states matter of factly now, "you have to learn to do all over again. Everything in the house has been reorganized so that I can handle things on a level. I just cannot tip my head down."

In the studio, all the tables are high off the floor so Marty can work without inclining her head. They are also on wheels so that she can move them around easily. "Everything is up," she points out; "everything is at eye level." To access the areas closer to the floor, such as the storage cupboards where her extensive collection of fabrics is kept, Bill devised low stools on wheels that Marty can sit on and move around easily.

The possibility that she could never work in miniatures again "is, was,

very real,'' she explains. ''And what would you do with the rest of your life? Well, I just had to learn how to do it all over again, and in an entirely new way.'' Her work, if possible, has become even better.

''For awhile I was really afraid,'' she admits, ''because it takes so much longer to do the dolls and there is so much pain involved, that the dolls I made wouldn't be as good, that the pain would interfere with the quality.''

Because of that pain, Marty works for short intervals and rests in between. ''I discovered that I spent my time between thinking it out more carefully,'' she notes.

Some of Marty's thinking time is spent working out on a cross country skiing machine in one corner of her studio. This machine provides her with an aggressive exercise program she can accomplish without moving her head. ''I researched it very carefully,'' she says proudly. ''I use my machine every day, and I work hard.''

Not knowing how long it will be until she is completely free of pain, or if

she ever will be, is very difficult sometimes, Marty admits, but ''I am not going to let this thing do me in.'' Besides, she adds, ''as an oil painter, as a portrait painter, I'm better'' than before the accident.

> *''I want the fabric to be right, I want the underwear to be right, and I want everything to be right.''*

Currently, Marty divides her time between painting with oils and creating porcelain dolls. ''I like to paint what I like to paint,'' Marty insists. ''I don't have to show in a gallery.'' She prefers not to, in fact. ''I like the feeling that I'm doing the best I know how to do, but I have not a competitive bone in my body. If you say the word, competition,'' she notes, ''I'm probably just not going to go.''

Still, she is pleased that she has the respect of the Boston art community

The little girl in this setting is dressed as authentically as possible. Of great help to Marty is her membership in the Costume Society, which enables her to examine many of the original garments.

for her larger paintings, and she considers it ''an honor'' to have been one of the first Guild Fellows selected by I.G.M.A. ''I always think it's an honor to be invited to a show and to be invited to teach at the School,'' Marty comments, adding, that ''I'm always pleased when somebody likes my work enough to buy it.

''When I started making the dolls, I realized, wasn't this interesting,'' Marty observes. ''I had been a fabric freak all my life; I know a lot about textiles, about fabrics. I had been a history buff all my life. I certainly sculpt; I've certainly done a lot of portraiture. Isn't this wrapping everything up together? Taking everything you love and putting it all in one basket?''

That's purely a rhetorical question in Marty's Saunders' case. It is all a part of what she is ''interested in, what I really love.''

Marty Saunders creates a doll

When Marty begins a miniature figure, she gathers all her reference materials, such as photos of the person she wishes to depict, costume references, shoe details, underwear plans, hair sketches and fabric samples. She makes a detailed drawing of the figure and puts it in a zip-lock bag along with all reference materials. She adds the fabrics, all laces, ribbons and trims. Then she is ready to sculpt.

PHOTO 1 (right top): Sculpting the head. This photo shows the plaster hat used to help control the moisture of the clay.

PHOTO 2 (right center): Marty uses the side of her hand to store the clay's differing moistures in preparation for addition to head.

PHOTO 3 (left): Adding the porcelain bow to the hair at the back of the head.

PHOTO 4 (far right): Sculpting the head, using a wooden tool. Shown in this photo are the various tools Marty uses: a wooden sculpture tool, X-Acto knife, various brushes in bistle and sable, dish of wet clay and water to add moisture.

PHOTO 5 (left): Sculpting with an X-Acto knife.

PHOTO 6 (above): A view of Marty's studio, showing her raised work table, the ironing board clamped to the table, and the studio's excellent light.

PHOTO 7 (left): The chest plate of the completed head is being hollowed out to receive the body.

PHOTO 8 (above): A finished but unfired head (left) is shown with a fired head. The head is fired at 2360% and shrinks 20% in the process.

PHOTO 9: The china paint pigment, in dry form, is ground on a tile, using fat oil of turpentine as a binder.

PHOTO 10: To paint the head, Marty uses a special brush made of badger hair bound in a chicken quill.

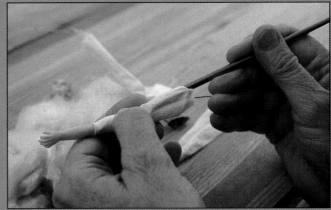

PHOTO 11 (left): Details are added in successive layers of china paint, using #6-0's sable brush. Each head is fired about 20 times.

PHOTO 12 (above): The finished fired, china-painted arm with wire expoxied into position. The arm casing is glued on and is being stuffed with kapok.

PHOTO 13: The stuffed legs are wired together in preparation for the body. The wires give the body articulation.

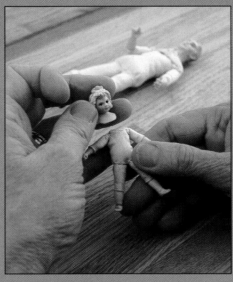

PHOTO 14 (above): The stuffed, assembled body is ready to have the head glued on.

PHOTO 15 (left): The hand-sewn underwear is being fitted to the figure.

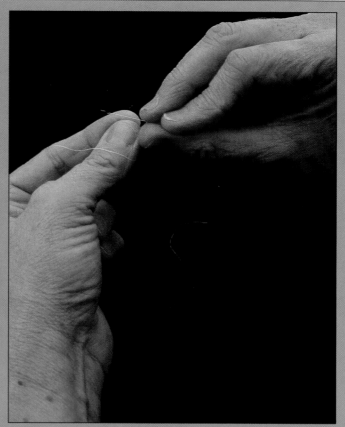

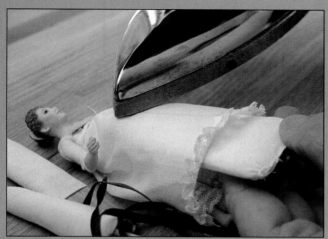

PHOTO 16: Marty designed special, miniature ironing boards to ease ironing right on the figure. The boards are small enough to reach into tiny places such as sleeves.

PHOTO 17: The figures are clothed by hand sewing. Here the silk thread is split into three strands before sewing a fine seam.

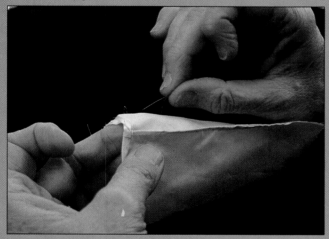

PHOTO 18 (above): The French back seam and a rolled hem are held in place with special fine pins.

PHOTO 19 (right): Finally, the taffeta skirt is ironed on the small board.

Noel & Pat Thomas

All experience is an arch, to build upon.
—Henry Brooks Adams

What makes a Thomas house a Thomas house? It is a rhetorical question with a complicated answer. "You have to have a vision," Noel Thomas believes, "so that you can foresee how something is going to work out. That's what you strive for. You don't accept any less than that."

A Thomas house has style, not in the universally-accepted sense of the word, but a very special style that has evolved in Noel and Pat's work over the 15 years or so that they have been creating miniature houses.

"If you are going to develop a style," Pat observes, "you are going to be very demanding of yourself," willing to make on-site construction changes when the work is straying from that original vision of what it is you have set out to accomplish. Noel calls his style: "A way of getting you to see what it is I am doing, forcing perspectives, forcing the eye to go further.'' He creates the illusion by ''breaking as many rules as I have to in order to achieve the effect I want. I think more than miniaturists, we are illusionists.''

A Thomas house creates the illusion for its viewers of a history, a past, a heritage that is impossible to mistake and complicated to achieve, but is built into the house step by step as the structure evolves from initial design onward. Both Noel and Pat share that vision from the beginning and work toward its completion as their common goal.

''People ask why Noel's designs are as good as they are,'' Pat notes, ''and it is because he was trained for it.'' Noel's art training took place in the 1950's at the Los Angeles Art Center, after ''a real Huck Finn childhood,'' as he describes it.

He grew up in Longview, Washington, where his father worked for the Long Bell Lumber Company before it became International Paper. ''Long Bell built the town of Longview in 1925,'' Noel explains, ''and my Dad was in on the beginning; he was part of the town being created.''

Noel's family lived a block from a man-made lake, and ''my fishing pole was stashed under the bridge,'' he remembers. ''I'd be coming home from school, two blocks from the school, across the lake, a rickety old wooden bridge, and there would be my fishing pole down there. I'd dig a worm out of the bank and take home fish, just right on my way home from school.'' His blue eyes sparkle as he vividly recalls this period in his life.

It was a childhood, idyllic in retrospect, that remains with him today. ''I'm a real small town, middle class kid,'' he insists, even though his career path took him into ''grey flannel suits, shirts with the perfect collar, Italian shoes, the whole thing. I did it, loved it, but it wasn't me.''

Noel was in his early teens when his parents divorced, his mother remarried, and Noel was given a choice. His stepfather had retired from the Navy, but ''when the Korean War broke out, they recalled him to active duty in San Diego to train recruits,'' Noel remembers, ''so my Mom gave me the big question: go along or stay here and live with my Dad. I said I'd go.

''I did all that '50's stuff in California,'' he continues, working during his high school years as night manager at a fast food restaurant to support his automobile. ''That was when you did all this custom work on your car,'' he explains, pointing out the photograph of it that hangs above his workbench today.

That was also a time when young men were being drafted into the Army. Noel was already in the reserves, he remembers, ''and getting really serious with this girl,'' who later became his first wife, when they decided he should go into active duty, postponing a marriage decision.

''Because I was a cook at Jack-in-the-Box, the fast food place, frying hamburgers, they made me a cook in the Army,'' Noel explains. He didn't have to carry a rifle, ''but I'd be out

A study of the partial view and detail of a Thomas house at right and below will reveal the illusion of the passage of time, with its ravages of weather and use, for which the couple's work is noted. Pat and Noel began building houses in 1974, when they moved close to the beach where they walk every morning (opposite page). Working together in their home studio, the Thomases enjoy a quality of life that can hardly be duplicated anywhere else.

on these damn bivouacs, sleeping in the mud under a truck, waiting for the troops to come back so I could feed them.''

It gave this young man some intense time for personal reflection, and what Noel thought about was a passing comment made years before by his eighth grade art teacher before he left Longview. ''Mrs. Johnson's voice popped right into my head,'' he relates. ''She said, if you don't think of anything else you'd like to do, when it comes time for college, you should go to the Los Angeles Art Center. You would do well,'' as Noel recalls the comment. He decided to take her ad-

vice, went on to a career in advertising, and did "do well." "Thank goodness for Mrs. Johnson," he laughs.

After his Art Center training was completed, Noel joined a prestigious New York City advertising agency, moved his family into a nearby suburb, and became "a hot-shot art director" at a time when advertising was a very exciting field to be involved in. "I don't mean to sound like I'm blowing my own horn," Noel insists. "I wasn't the only one, but I was in with them, and I was very good with concept. I could come up with new ways of seeing things. I enjoyed my job, oh, tremendously," he continues, for the next nine years.

What he did not enjoy was the commuting, the cold weather, "the abrasive manner of some of the people. I found myself becoming a little like them," he believes. It was time for a change. It seemed to be the right time for a move back to California, and Noel was offered a job in an agency that was in the process of changing its direction, of trying to become more creative.

Noel was one of several New York advertising men hired "to come out here and turn this thing around," he explains. "Well, it lasted about six months. They weren't ready for that creative stuff. It frightened the clients. It wasn't worked out well enough in advance." As the others left, Noel realized "I couldn't stay either." Nor did he want to go back to New York.

> *"If you are going to develop a style, you are going to be very demanding of yourself."*

Instead, he went to work for a production company as a film director, producing commercials for television. But advertising had already begun to lose its appeal for Noel. He stayed with it, though, for the next half-dozen years during which time his marriage ended, and he met an attractive, young copywriter from New York.

Although born in New York, Pat was "raised in Massachusetts, in a 200-year-old farmhouse. My parents were always restoring that house," she claims. "I learned to strip paint at a very young age." Pat went to Skidmore College in Saratoga Springs, New York, where "I was a Drama major and an English minor," she explains, "a regular, Liberal Arts education, which I was encouraged to get." She enjoyed theater and her drama courses, learned to build sets and scenery, and, after graduation, went back to New York "and attempted to continue my acting career," she notes, "which was not meant to be." A few years later, Pat moved to Los Angeles and "got into advertising as a copywriter."

Noting that they often get letters from young people who say they want to do exactly what the Thomases are doing now, Pat says, "I know we drive them crazy with our answer: First, you go to school and get a good Liberal Arts background. Then you specialize in whatever you want to specialize in, or are good in, and you work for about 15 years in that career. Then when you've got enough accumulated experience, you

Their friendly, old dog Sunshine watches as Noel and Pat Thomas pose for the camera in their living room (left). The black stove keeps this level warm on damp, chilly days and helps heat the adjacent studio. When they first moved here from Los Angeles, many of the local people they met were curious enough about them, and their work, to stop by to see them at any hour of the day. Noel and Pat had to gently convince them that they really were working, and needed uninterrupted time. Now, as each house is completed and ready for delivery, the Thomases have an open house so all their local friends can see it. Two striped cats also share the Thomases' home. The staircase (top), serves as a handy resting place for a few of the large collection of books Noel and Pat avidly read and use for research.

start building dollhouses for a profession,'' she concludes.

"But, that's how we did it,'' Pat claims. "All of the things that we did brought us to where we are now. If we had started in our 20's,'' she believes, "we wouldn't have been able to do the kind of work we did when we first started out in 1974. It's interesting, the coming together of all the things each of us has done over the years.''

Noel and Pat had both become somewhat disenchanted with their careers in advertising, "it wasn't one of the more creative periods in advertising then,'' she observes, when Noel asked if she "would like to come up here and take a look at where I grew up,'' he recalls. "I was seriously thinking about getting out of LA, thinking about moving up here. So I brought her up and she fell in love with it.''

They had started to plan the move when they decided to build a dollhouse for Noel's daughter, Robin, who was about 10 years old. "It was a typical, first dollhouse,'' Pat insists, and were at work on their second house, deciding that "of course, we could do much better,'' when a friend gave them a newspaper article about someone who was building dollhouses for a living, "and there was a market for them,'' Pat recalls. "We were foolish enough to say, oh, let's do that. We'll build dollhouses for a living.''

"We could certainly try it,'' Noel recalls deciding pragmatically, "and if it doesn't work, if we find out within a year or two, we can still get back into advertising.'' As it turned out, their advertising careers were permanently behind them, and a new career was about to begin. It was Spring, 1974.

"Luckily, the economy was in good shape at the time,'' Pat recalls, and "we were early into the market. There weren't a lot of people building dollhouses, and miniatures collecting was just beginning its resurgence.''

Seaview, Washington, where they chose to settle, is a tiny beach community on the Pacific Coast that had vivid and happy memories for Noel. "My Dad discovered the beach down here when we were little kids,'' he recalls. "He was a frustrated archi-

tect, the same as I am, but he had worked with real materials and he built a little weekend place here at the beach.''

It seemed a logical place for Noel and Pat to escape to, after the frantic pace of Los Angeles. Not exactly in the mainstream, Seaview is some 130 miles from Portland, Oregon, over a mostly two-lane, twisting but scenic road, part of which traces the route of the Lewis and Clark expedition. Seaview is a town with a distinct quality of life, a certain ambiance, a town that changes only gradually and reluctantly. And, at the time the Thomases moved there, "the cost of living was extremely low,'' Pat points out. "We were able to live on very little; even now we are able to live on a very low income. If we lived in the city, we never would have made it.''

> *"We were foolish enough to say, oh, let's do that. We'll build dollhouses for a living.''*

Noel and Pat rented a house built in the 1920's with an option to buy, "the driest house that was available to rent'' that wet spring, Noel laughs. "It was a good year to be looking at real estate because you really knew what was going to happen,'' Pat adds. "This lot was high and dry.'' Probably built as a summer cottage, the house is not what Noel describes as "serious. Most of the houses around here weren't serious houses,'' he insists, from an architect's point of view.

It is a house, though, with undeniable charm. A vintage woodstove in the living room provides the heat. A trap-door at the top of the stairway to the bedrooms can be closed to keep the heat downstairs. Their studio, off the living room, is the only structural change the Thomases have needed to make to the house. They doubled its size, after working in the smaller space for several years, and added baseboard heat in that room. The house contains an eclectic assortment of furnishings, including Pat's piano, the Oriental rugs Noel admires, books in every available niche, and collectibles of the period of the house. It seems as comfortable and inviting as ... well, one of the miniature houses Noel and Pat have built.

"So, living where we live has made all the difference," Pat believes, both in the type of work they are doing and in the way they have chosen to live. "When you're mad at work, or you're mad at business, or you're mad at each other, it's so pretty here," she continues. "There's the beach," where they take a walk every morning, "there's some green, things like that, to keep your sanity. When things get bad, at least we're in a nice place and have a lot of friends. It's a nice community," she feels.

Both the Thomases are involved with their community. Pat, with her interests in music, has been the organizer and chairman of an annual music festival. The Water Music Festival is now in its third successful year. Noel designed the logo for it "right out of my Art Center training," he comments. Noel is active in the Meals on Wheels program, taking his turn once a week to deliver a hot meal to older residents who are homebound. There are meetings to attend, but "it has been a nice thing, to be able to add a little bit to the quality of life here," Pat believes. Even so, "we do have to get off this peninsula once in awhile," Noel observes.

The first time they left, after the move to Seaview, was to go back to

Elements of this full-size house (top) a block or so from the Thomases' have been copied and incorporated into their miniature houses. Noel and Pat have built over thirty miniature structures. Not all of them are houses. Some are called "character buildings" and some are "fragments." A view of some of the tools and materials in the studio is shown above, with Noel at work, reflected in the mirror on the wall. "People ask why Noel's designs are as good as they are. It's because he was trained in it," Pat explains. "He's not just a carpenter putting things together."

California to a N.A.M.E. National Houseparty, with their first exhibited dollhouse. "We felt confident that we were doing pretty good work," Pat says in retrospect, "and we put our house in the exhibit room. It looked pretty good with the work that was there, we thought. So, we went away and came back the next morning to find that, in the middle of the night, Jim Marcus had arrived with his Russian Embassy and put it right next to ours. And that was the last anyone saw of our house," she concludes, matter-of-factly.

It was a rude awakening for these two who had "always done what we felt like doing, and then made it work out," Pat admits. "We had thought, hey, we're in advertising, we know everything, we're city kids, we can do this. No, we couldn't. We had to come home and figure out how to do it, do our homework."

Might it have crossed their minds at that point to go back into advertising? "We wouldn't admit it to one another," Noel agrees. "We came home scared, and it was great because it made us respect the business more,"

Pat insists. It was a lesson they have never forgotten.

"Jim befriended us at that show and he has become a very good friend of ours," Noel continues. "We correspond via cassette all the time, and we have a running dialogue. He knows exactly what I'm doing and I know what he's doing. We're not in direct competition for sales, but we keep poking and prodding one another to explore, experiment," he says.

"We both knew, right off the bat, that we didn't want to build the same kind of houses Jim was doing," Pat explains, "mainly because we didn't have them around here. We needed something we could identify with, that we could live with and understand," she comments. The Thomas style was about to be born.

"There was one project there that helped me establish a style," Noel remembers. "I didn't have a style; I was just making a house. I didn't have an approach." That project was a "water tower dwelling," he says, "and inside was this little apartment full of nooks and crannies, interesting little bathroom fixtures, plumbing

with water stains on the walls, and I looked in there and thought, boy, this is real. Very interesting. Now we're starting to hum. Now I'm starting to find what I like in this crazy businesses of miniatures and dollhouses, what it is that appeals to me. I will always have an affinity for that project," Noel insists, "because it really set the direction for me. I knew then what I wanted to do, what I needed to do, to start making some decent houses."

It was also the beginning of their full-time working partnership. Until then Noel had been the primary dollhouse builder and Pat had helped support them by working in a hardware

In this spacious studio (above), Noel and Pat go to work every day. Noel creates the design and draws the plans for each house at his desk in this room, a process which might take a month. "I'm friends with most of the local carpenters and architects," he comments, "and we do have a good one on the peninsula. He lets me see what he's doing, consults with me. He respects my eye, even though I'm not an architect or a builder. I enjoy that."

store. "Then it made more sense for me to be home full-time," she says. Today their division of labor is "all over the lot," as Noel puts it. "She is more and more understanding of the overall concept, and has many more positive suggestions, thoughts that are right on target."

As they talk about their life and work this day, Pat, seated on a stool pulled up to the large table holding their current project, is meticulously laying a complicated brick pattern on the terrace at the back of the house. Noel is applying a cement mixture to a front corner. Classical music provides the background; there is a tape deck in the living room.

Both can handle almost all of the work involved in each project, but Pat leaves the stained glass detail to Noel who had just a few, short lessons in the craft before he left Los Angeles so long ago, developing his own miniaturization techniques. Noel also does all the wood cutting "and he does it by hand," Pat marvels. "We don't have the tools that most people have because Noel doesn't need them. It

drives me crazy," she laughs.

Noel trusts a saber saw for most work, a gift from Jim Marcus. "I can make a darned near perfect, straight line with it," Noel boasts, when he wants or needs to, although a perfect, straight plane is not to be found in many Thomas houses. "When I want to have a little sag here, the wall lean a little there, I'll cut it at a slight angle, so it's there," he explains.

"We want to keep our reputation, and in order to keep it, we have to keep bettering ourselves."

It is one of the many techniques Noel and Pat teach in their classes. "We do enjoy teaching," Pat insists. "It's about the only contact we have with people in the miniatures world." Each year at the I.G.M.A. School in Castine, Maine, and occasionally at other times, Noel and Pat teach their techniques, "how we get our work to

look the way it looks," Noel relates.

"But we also try to teach them to make their work look like their work," Pat adds. "You've got to develop your own style." Some of their students are more amenable than others. "The hardest students we have to work with are the totally precisioned people," Pat explains, "because we don't work that way." Some of them become converts to the Thomas methods, but some find they don't like it.

What every student does get during the class is a bottle of what Noel graphically refers to as "bug juice," a special formula with such obscure ingredients that it would be virtually impossible to duplicate. When it is used on most types of wood, it causes the wood to acquire a patina that

The prototype for a Guild School class sits on the work table in the Thomases' studio. Details for this cottage that Noel and Pat helped their students construct are shown on the opposite page. Of this house Pat says, "You get a nice feeling of accomplishment, working on a small piece."

duplicates years of aging. Noel has been told that gunsmiths used it, or a formula similar to this one, to darken the wooden stocks of their guns. He uses it, with much success, on ''just about any piece of wood that you haven't hidden underneath four coats of varnish,'' he explains, pointing out the shingles on the roof of a little cottage built as a class prototype. ''They have a silvery sheen to them,'' he notes, ''like weathered, old shingles.''

That little cottage could be on any one of the side streets in Seaview, if it were in full size. It is a current and graphic example of how the Thomas style has evolved over the years. ''Every aspect of what we do, builds on our style,'' Noel believes. ''We like being innovative,'' Pat adds. ''We want to keep our reputation, and in order to keep it, we have to keep bettering ourselves.''

When artisans can do something as well as the Thomases can, the chances are very good that attempts will be made to copy them. ''We were very upset about copying for a long time,'' Pat admits, ''and didn't know how to deal with it, but finally decided we can't worry about it. You have to take it as flattery,'' she believes, ''and just realize you have to work a little harder. And you have to keep changing directions.''

Noel and Pat's current project represents just such a change in direction. ''The interesting aspect with this kind of house,'' Pat notes, ''is that it is designed after the work of two architecture geniuses, Greene and Greene. It's trying to be as good as they are, trying to think the way they thought and do things the way they did. That is what adds time to a project like this. They are always in our minds.''

Pictured on this page are details of the ''South Bend'' house. ''I'm using all the elements of the period, but I'm in control of what the outcome is,'' Noel says of this Victorian house. Years-old vacuum cleaner dust is the secret of that musty aroma, Pat explains. ''It's what attics and things really smell like.'' The effect of deterioration in the foundation of this house (far right) is achieved by what Noel calls ''secondary distressing.''

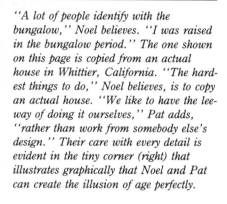

"A lot of people identify with the bungalow," Noel believes. "I was raised in the bungalow period." The one shown on this page is copied from an actual house in Whittier, California. "The hardest things to do," Noel believes, is to copy an actual house. "We like to have the leeway of doing it ourselves," Pat adds, "rather than work from somebody else's design." Their care with every detail is evident in the tiny corner (right) that illustrates graphically that Noel and Pat can create the illusion of age perfectly.

Noel designed the house to resemble the Gamble House in Pasadena, California, "but I'm just taking the flavor of the Gamble House and working it into the miniature," he explains. The Gamble House in full size is 8,000 square feet which would be "overwhelming," he feels, if constructed exactly to scale.

"I have become more flexible over the years," Noel continues, when it comes to scale. Although working essentially in inch-to-a-foot scale, "nothing is scaled down an inch to a foot and looks right in miniature," he feels. "It just doesn't." Without even thinking consciously about it, Noel's art training comes to the fore. "This house is going to end up looking like a whole lot more house than it's actually going to be in square feet," he goes on.

To achieve this illusion, the tiles are slightly smaller, the bricks are just under standard size, probably closer to 7/8ths or even 3/4ths of an inch

equals one foot. "You want the impression that you're viewing it as you would a real house," Pat observes. "That's why you have to work around the scale, to make it look right."

Work of this caliber and detail goes slowly, but their customers are willing to wait for their houses. "It takes us more time now," Pat explains, "because we've gotten into more detail work. But we've found that it's worth it to us, and to our customers. We've never had a customer unhappy."

Although they have built some 36 structures over the years, it now takes Noel and Pat approximately one year to build a miniature house. "When we're through with the

piece," Noel comments, "I want to feel just as good about this one we've just finished as we felt about the last one. There is an incredible 'rush' there, a wonderful, satisfying thing that goes on," a priceless feeling, he adds. "There is no way to compromise the work." And, Pat observes, "we have the satisfaction of knowing that we have created something new in every house, and have done all the things we wanted to do, have done the work just the way we want it to be."

The design and the vision, the careful workmanship and the illusion of its heritage, these then are the components that make a Thomas house truly a Thomas house.

A visit to Noel and Pat Thomas' studio

PHOTO 1: Prior to building any project a great deal of time is put into designing and drawing up three-dimensional plans for each of the Thomases' houses.

PHOTO 2: Pat is working in her corner of the studio, with shelves full of materials for projects present and future.

PHOTO 3: Noel is at the scroll saw cutting pieces for the Hawaiian Fruit Stand prototype.

PHOTO 4: Pat is building fruit crates for the Hawaiian Fruit Stand, which was built for the 1987 NAME Houseparty cruise around the Hawaiian islands.

PHOTO 5: Noel is working on diagrams for the Hawaiian Fruit Stand workshop.

Glass by Francis Whittemore.

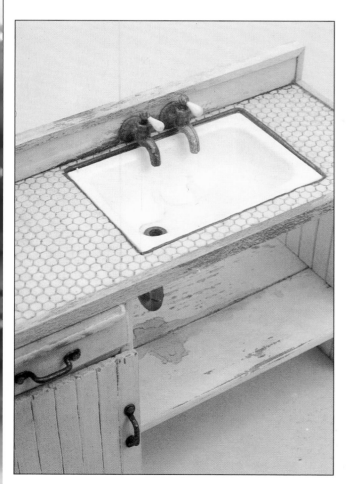

Kitchen sink by Noel Thomas.

Stove by Noel Thomas

Francis Whittemore

By the work one knows the workman.
—Jean De La Fontaine

The creating of it goes back to early civilizations. It is dark, it is light. It is opaque, it is clear. It reflects, it contains. It is fragile, it is strong. It is everywhere, and it is glass.

Although manufactured glass had been in existence for many years, the art of glassblowing is believed to have been invented in the first century B.C. by Syrian craftsman who used a process that is essentially the same today as it was then. It is an art that has endured through countless generations into modern times. Today, there is an elite group of perhaps only half a dozen glassblowers in the United States who are acknowledged to be the best at what they do. Francis Whittemore is one of them.

"Glassblowers are sort of strange people at times," Frank believes, "because they are the last of the independent craftsmen who are still needed in modern industry. It's very difficult to reduce glassmaking to an automatically-controlled machine," he continues. "Complex things are generally made by people." Frank

knows a great deal about the making of glass because he has been a glassblower for 50 years.

Frank was born in New Jersey and lived in the Boston area during his growing up years. His father, trained as a chemist, was a Senior Master in the Boston Public Schools where he taught chemistry and science. When he was 17 and in high school, Frank first became intrigued with glassblowing. "A friend of mine got interested in playing with glass," he recalls, "and bought some glass straws. I decided that looked sort of interesting and tried the same thing."

With the simple equipment they were using, "you couldn't do much but make bottles," Frank reminisces, "little, round bubbles on the end of a tube. My father suggested that I go over to one of the apparatus houses in Cambridge, one of the places that sold to the University, and get a decent burner and blower and tubing," he continues. "I found out that blowers were expensive so I used the wrong end of a little hand vacuum cleaner for the air source which worked very well for years," he recalls now.

Along with the more sophisticated equipment he found at the apparatus supplier, Frank was able to watch professional glassblowers at work. "A lot of people helped me," he remembers, by letting him watch what they were doing. In some cases it was a technique he had already worked out by himself at home, but

he never let them know that. "I really never apprenticed anywhere," he admits. "I taught myself how to blow glass and within six months I was selling things to local gift shops."

The first glass he made to sell was what is still referred to as "cabinet pieces," Frank explains. "Miniatures, but not in scale. People collected pitchers and vases, and then I started making animals, too. Colored tubing was somewhat more available then." He still has a supply of it. "It's a good thing I'm a packrat," Frank smiles, "because you can't get colored glass anymore; you just can't buy it."

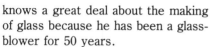

"Glassblowers are sort of strange people at times."

At about this time Frank became a member of the Society of Arts and Crafts in Boston. "It was an organization of professional craftsmen," Frank comments. "Very high standards, juried. People could order everything at their showroom on Newbury Street from a gold tea service to a miniature perfume bottle, and I made that." He was also spending time at Boston's Museum of Fine Arts, studying the glass in the mu-

"It's always a lot of fun to have people appreciate what you do," Frank Whittemore feels. "I think people are much more confident in collecting miniatures because they are collecting things they are familiar with. People know what a decanter is, what goblets are, so they come in and they know what they want." Frank makes over a dozen different styles of decanter such as the classic style pictured in the photos above left and center. "Glassblowers are like everybody else," he feels. "Some have a good sense of design, and some of them don't." He makes his own striped glass for pieces like the footed compote shown above right, with a striped bowl and crystal base and stem.

seum's collection, and had made friends with several of the curators by the time the Thorne Rooms arrived to be put on exhibit after their display at the World's Fair in New York.

"Several pieces had been damaged in shipping," Frank recalls, "and they had gotten someone else in to repair them who hadn't done a decent job. So the curators called me in. I guess I was about 18 at the time." When he got there, Frank was not allowed to touch the rooms until he was verified by the woman who was in charge of the exhibit. "She went into the next room," he laughs, "called up the curator, and said, are you sure this kid can do it?" Frank remembers repairing chandeliers with glass beads, and "gluing a couple of pieces of furniture back together," he says. "It was a lot of fun getting behind the

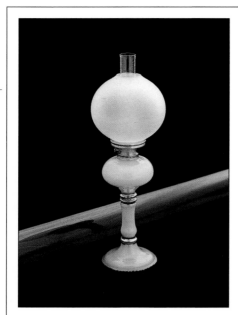

Full-size paperweights such as the ones shown here (left center and lower right, opposite page) have gained Frank Whittemore the deserved reputation as one of only half a dozen superb glassblowers in the United States. "Nobody in the rest of the world is making weights as good as they're being made in this country," he believes, "at all." Pictured at top left is a miniature lamp of luminescent ivory glass, typical of the Victorian period, ca. 1860. Other period glass is shown in the photo at lower left. The famous Tiffany lily shape is on the left. All three pieces are typical of the work of Louis Comfort Tiffany in iridescent or "favrile" glass.

scenes and seeing how the rooms were done."

When Frank was ready to go to college, he entered Harvard University with the Class of 1945, intending to become a chemical engineer, although he recalls being told at the time that "my strong points lay in other directions." If he had a chance to do it again, he says now, I'd major in humanities or something to do with languages. I speak French. I spoke a passable German. I used to speak a little Spanish, and I knew some Russian." Languages, he recalls, came easily to him then.

While he was at Harvard, Frank signed up with the student employment agency as a glassblower willing to give demonstrations. "I would take my equipment and make all sorts of silly things," he reminisces, "like swans, which I disliked, and blow half-sized pitchers so that people could see what I was doing." Frank was in demand at schools, church bazaars, and women's club meetings, demonstrating his craft and selling the items he made. Often his income was $50 a week, "a lot of money then," he observes.

Frank had to leave Harvard in the summer of 1942 when he was drafted into the Army in World War II. "I spent three years in the service," he remembers, "about a year in Germany and a year in France. I was outside Paris for almost seven months as a medic in a pipeline company."

When he came home, Frank decided not to return to Harvard. His mother, widowed, had moved to Delaware so he decided to settle

there, too. "I had had it with regimentation," he comments about that period, "so I tried to start the glassblowing business again, but it didn't work," at least as a full-time occupation. He went to work in a laboratory at DuPont, and continued to give glassblowing demonstrations in his spare time.

> *"She went into the next room, called up the curator, and said, are you sure this kid can do it?"*

Frank was giving a demonstration at a church bazaar when he met Lois. "I was blowing glass and selling things," he remembers. "She was watching me, and that's how I met her." Married in 1955, Frank and Lois now have three daughters, two sons, and one grandson. After going back to school for her RN, Lois works as a nurse, specializing in geriatrics, handles the business' paperwork, "and beats me with a stick occasionally to get me organized," Frank laughs.

When he went to work at DuPont, Frank also "decided that I would see what was going on in the miniature field," he remembers, and subscribed to *Hobbies* magazine "which was the only place that I knew of that had a column on miniatures." This led to his association with Joseph H. Grey in Chicago, starting in 1946 and continuing for about ten years. "Grey bought steadily from me," Frank recalls. "He was a good customer and an interesting individual." The two finally met in the early 1960's when Frank went to Chicago for a scientific seminar. "I went to his home and saw his collection," Frank continues.

In the mid-1950's Frank stopped making miniatures in any quantity when, along with his full-time job at DuPont which by now was as a scientific glass blower, he was asked to do glass work part-time on a research program with chemistry graduate students. It started out taking just two or three evenings a week and eventually became an every-weekend endeavor. "But it was very interesting work," he recalls; "it was different."

Pointing out that "glassblowers are always looking for jobs," Frank decided to move to Philco Corporation and the family relocated to Lansdale, Pennsylvania, where they still live. When Philco closed in the 1960's, "I went into business for myself making paperweights," Frank explains. It was his work with paperweights that led to his reputation as one of the half-dozen best glassblowers in the United States today.

"I started making weights in 1961," Frank relates, "and the reason I did was because I was teaching evenings in a vocational-technical school. A number of the students were learning scientific glassblowing during the day, and the school wanted them to be able to go out and get summer jobs." Frank's task was to teach these students how to blow decorative glass. "Some of them did very well at it," he recalls. Although he did not realize it until one of his students pointed it out to him, the school's brochure listed paperweights as one of the techniques Frank would teach. It had not occurred to him until then to make them, but he quickly became proficient enough to make Millville Rose paperweights, and eventually became an expert at the work himself.

It was his expertise that led to an invitation to speak at the Paperweight Collectors' Association in 1971, and while he was there, Frank met Andre Vulliet who was at that time a vice president of Baccarat Crystal. He told Frank that the company was interested in paperweights and asked if Frank would go to Baccarat in France to help them get started. "I went over

to Baccarat and spent a month each year there for about five years," Frank explains.

The company paid Lois' expenses as well and the schedule allowed some extra time for sightseeing, "but with five kids at home," Frank notes, "it was a little difficult to be away too long. One year we took all five of them to France.

"It's a major crystal house," Frank remarks about Baccarat. "They call themselves 'the crystal of Kings'. Surprisingly enough, I never found out how many glassblowers they had. They ran two major furnaces, a fair amount of small furnaces, and a number of tank furnaces; sometimes two shifts. It's a big factory." Frank's former fluency in French came back to him during his work at Baccarat. "If you're trying to give someone

The tobacco jar pictured above, right, is made of ivory opaque glass. A Whittemore tea set with cup and saucers in light blue opaque glass is shown at center right. The hexagon shape is achieved by blowing the glass in a mold. When Frank makes a tea pot, he attaches the spout first and then the handle because it is easier to make minor adjustments to the placement of the handle.

technical information,'' he notes, ''you have to give it right. In ordinary conversation, you can slip a little bit and it doesn't matter.''

While he was at the convention, held in Beverly Hills, California, Frank had what he terms with amusement, ''an interesting experience. I was coming down in the elevator to go to a meeting. It was getting a little late, Lois had already gone down, and this 'grande dame' stepped into the elevator and looked at me. Without even asking me if I spoke French, she asked, 'Are you married?' When I said I was,'' Frank continues, ''she asked if I had daughters. When I said I did, she turned around with her back to me and said, 'Zip me up!', and I did.''

Frank remembers the work he did with the glassblowers in France as a very positive experience. ''They were tremendous people,'' he says. ''They treated me very, very well.'' During the rest of those years with

> *''[Lois] beats me with a stick occasionally to get me organized.''*

Baccarat, Frank was creating his own paperweights, building his reputation for making ''good quality weights, probably the most difficult thing you could do in glassblowing,'' he notes.

Pictured above is a colorful and delicate array of Whittemore glass. The mug shown at lower right against a background of colored glass rods has been "irudized so that it has a bronze surface to it," Frank explains. "Irudizing is what Tiffany did to the surface of his glass. They were trying to imitate Greco-Roman glass and came up with something quite different, but interesting." Also shown below is a Tiffany lamp (center) that would be a prized addition to a miniature Art Nouveau room setting. Each Whittemore decanter has an authentic glass stopper (below, right).

''I thought it was very challenging, and rewarding in all directions,'' Frank recalls, until he had an accident and injured the tendons in both arms.

He could no longer work on the

heavy paperweights. "It was a scarey thing," Frank confesses. "I couldn't do anything." For a time, the yarn shop Lois operated then supported the family. When Frank could work again, it seemed logical to go back to making miniatures. "I had been looking at the miniature field anyway, casually keeping track of it," and occasionally making some scaled miniatures, Frank explains. "I never really stopped making them.

"The thing is," he continues, "I made very good miniatures years ago, but I'm making much better miniatures now than I've ever made. Fortunately," he feels, "I'm still learning, still figuring things out, which is encouraging. That makes it very interesting."

> *"No matter how good you are, or how long you've been working, you're never completely positive that you are going to finish what you start."*

Frank has been exhibiting and selling his glassware at miniatures shows all over the country for ten years. "I think that people in the miniatures business are right across the board pretty friendly, pretty interesting," he observes. "Very interesting to talk to, and pleasant. I haven't quite figured out why it attracts people like that. I suppose there could be some deep, psychological reason, but the important thing is that it works."

At home in his workshop, miniature bottles about one-quarter of an inch

"The kind of work I do is called 'lamp work,' " Frank explains. "Lamp work refers to the technique of using burners and tubing to make things." Creating the miniature glass flowers for the centers of full-size paperweights such as the one shown at right "was good training for making miniatures," Frank confides. "You have to be very precise."

*"One of the most difficult things to do,"
Frank explains, "is to make a flat, blown
piece, like a plate. That is true in full-size
or in miniature, and nobody realizes that.
Only a glassblower recognizes that because
it is something very technical, very specific
to the glassblowing business."*

tall are "probably the easiest thing that I make," Frank believes. One of the most difficult is a footed pyramid of three cake plates in graduated sizes, topped by a footed bowl. Believed to have originated in England about 1750, the pyramid found its way to Williamsburg where Frank saw it. "The plates are very hard to make because they're flat," he explains. "I've got it pretty well worked out how to put them together, but I still lose some because you've got this large, flat surface with a small stem on it, and you have to keep it hot all over so you can work on it. If you get it too hot," he continues, "the center gets soft and it cocks. If you don't get

it hot enough, it cracks."

It is in working out the most difficult problems that Frank's long experience with glass comes to the fore. "One of the things you have to do," he counsels, "is to learn very quickly how to put things together. You learn to do things right the first time, because you don't want to play with it and try to save it which sometimes takes more time than it does to make another one. If it's a very complicated piece and you have a lot of time in it," he continues, "you have to know how to save it." Or when to throw it away and start over.

"No matter how good you are," Frank feels, "or how long you've

been working, you're never completely positive that you are going to finish what you start." Good glassblowers, though, can make judgments very quickly about what is possible to make and what is not. "It becomes second nature," Frank believes, just as the protection of their "trade secrets" become. "There are always some things glassblowers will not show other people," he adds.

If he were going to advise anyone considering glassblowing as a career, Frank observes, "you have to have talent to figure out how to put things together if you are going to do things that are different. In a sense, that isn't something you learn. Then you take advantage of all the experience that is around," he continues; "see everybody that you can who is working. And you teach yourself how to do things." But, most of all, Frank feels, "you have to have an innate talent to handle the glass."

It is this innate, natural talent to handle glass that has allowed Francis Whittemore to become the master that he is, of an art form that goes back over 2,000 years.

Frank Whittemore at work

PHOTO 1 (left): Frank is "pulling a point" — drawing the tube down so it can be handled more easily. The tube (in Frank's right hand) has been heated. The rod is in his left hand. After heating the tube is pulled.
PHOTO 2 (above): Heating to pull a second point.

PHOTO 3 (left): Blowing the bulb on a pitcher.
PHOTO 4 (right): Taking the bottom point off.

PHOTO 5: (left): Flattening the bottom of the pitcher.
PHOTO 6 (right): Attaching glass rod as a temporary handle.

PHOTO 7 (above left): Flaring the neck.
PHOTO 8 (above right): Applying the handle.

PHOTO 9 (far left): Making the pour spout.
PHOTO 10 (left): Annealing the pitcher so it doesn't crack. This relieves the strain on the glass.

PHOTO 11 (right): The finished pitcher.
PHOTO 12 (far right): Getting ready to pull a spout.

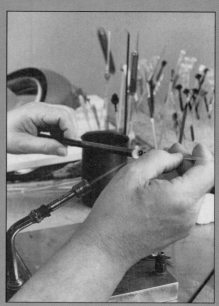

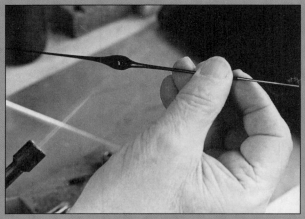

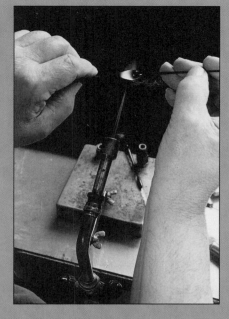

PHOTO 13 & 14 (above & right): Making a glass slipper.

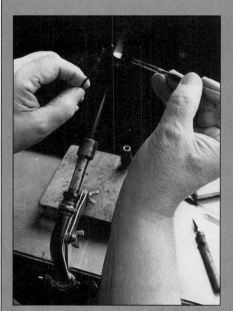

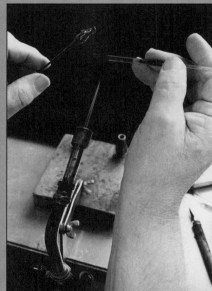

PHOTO 15 (far left): Preparing to attach heel.
PHOTO 16 (left): The heel is on.

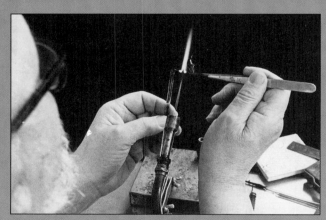

PHOTO 17: Finishing the heel, and removing the glass rod.

PHOTO 18: The annealing oven, which increases the temperature of the finished pieces to remove stress, making the pieces less fragile.